ROCK CHARTS
GUITAR 2004

The Biggest Hits, The Greatest Artists

Deluxe *Annual* Edition

MW01165863

Project Manager: Aaron Stang
Production Coordinator: Karl Bork
Art Layout and Design: Debbie Johns

CONTENTS

ALONE I BREAK

Words and Music by
KORN

All gtrs. are 7-string gtrs. tuned down 1 1/2 steps:

⑦ = G♯ ③ = E
⑥ = C♯ ② = G♯
⑤ = F♯ ① = C♯
④ = B

Moderately ♩ = 78
Intro:

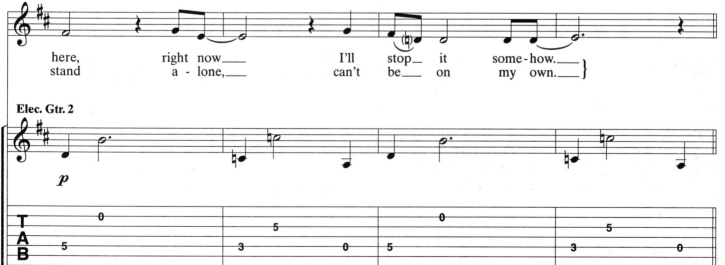

1. Pick me up,___ been bleed-ing too long.___ Right___
2. Shut me off,___ I'm read-y, too heart stops.___ I___

here, right now___ I'll stop___ it some-how.___
stand a - lone,___ can't be___ on my own.___}

Pre-chorus:

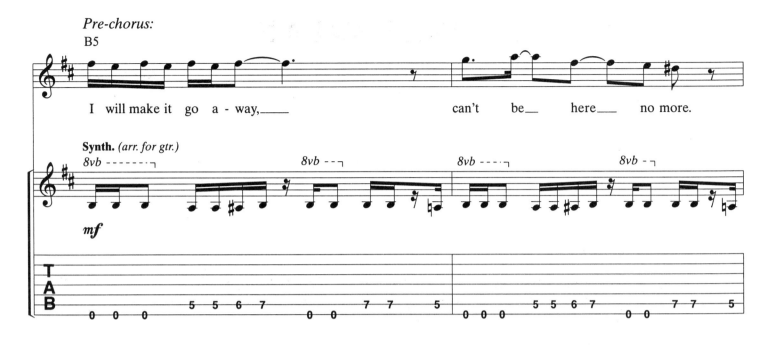

B5

I will make it go a-way,_____ can't be_ here_ no more.

Synth. *(arr. for gtr.)*

mf

Seems this is the on-ly way,_____ I will_ soon_ be gone.

Bm   Am

These feel - ings_ will_____ be gone.

Elec. Gtr. 3

p

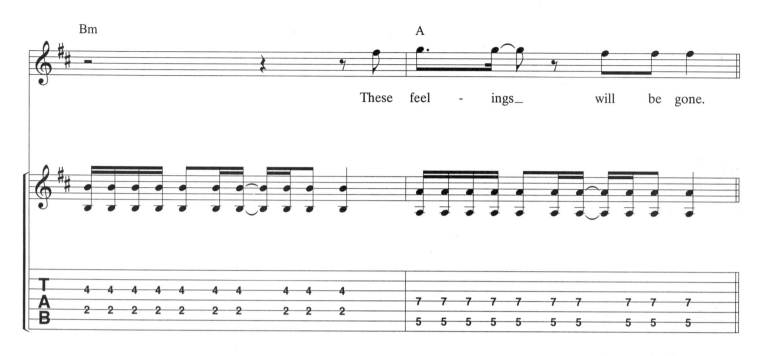

These feel - ings__ will be gone.

Chorus:

Now I see__ the times__ they change,__ leav - ing us__ it seems__ so strange.__

Elec. Gtr. 2
Rhy. Fig. 2

Elec. Gtr. 4
Rhy. Fig. 2A

8

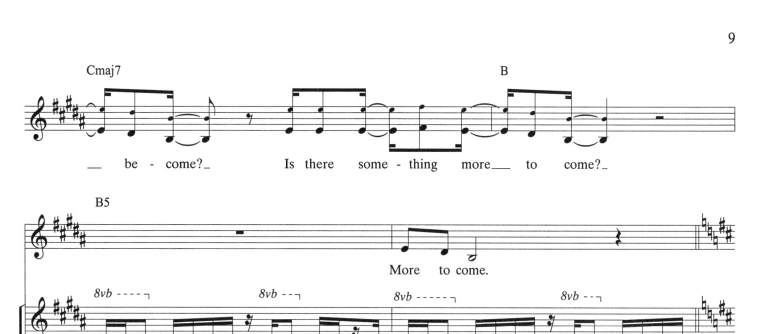

Chorus:
w/Rhy. Figs. 2 *(Elec. Gtr. 2)* **& 2A** *(Elec. Gtr. 4), both 2 times*

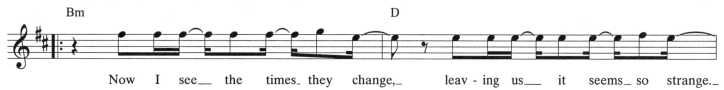

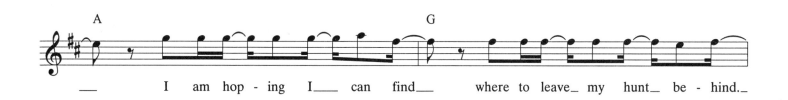

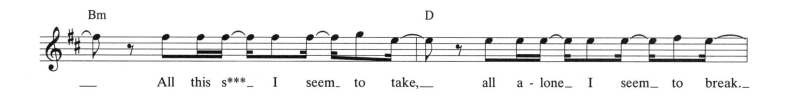

BREATHE

Words and Music by
MICHELLE BRANCH and
JOHN SHANKS

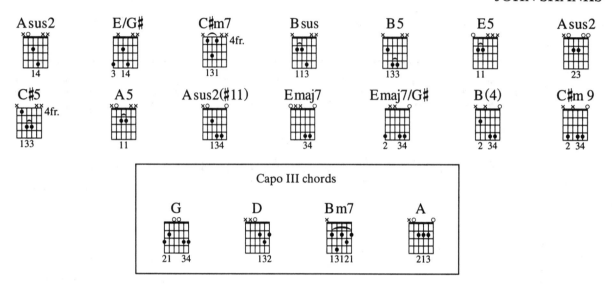

*Acous. Gtr. 1 & Elec. Gtrs. 1 & 3 Capo I
*Acous. Gtr. 2 & Elec. Gtr. 2 Capo III

Moderately ♩ = 116
Intro:

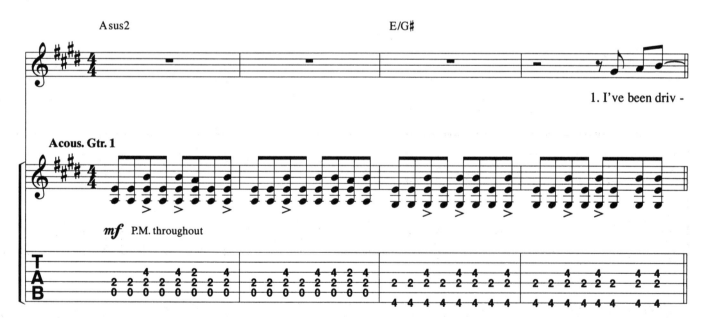

*Tune slightly sharp to match recording.
Music sounds 1/2 step (plus) higher that written.

Verse:

Asus2
**(G)

E/G#
(D)

Acous. Gtr. 2
on repeats

Cont. rhy. simile

- ing for___ an hour,___ just___ talk - ing to___ the rain.___
___ me one___ good rea - son,___ tell me why___ I___ should stay.___

3. *See additional lyrics*

Elec. Gtr. 3
(clean-tone)
on D.S.

hold throughout

**Chords in parentheses represent gtr. capoed at the 3rd fret.

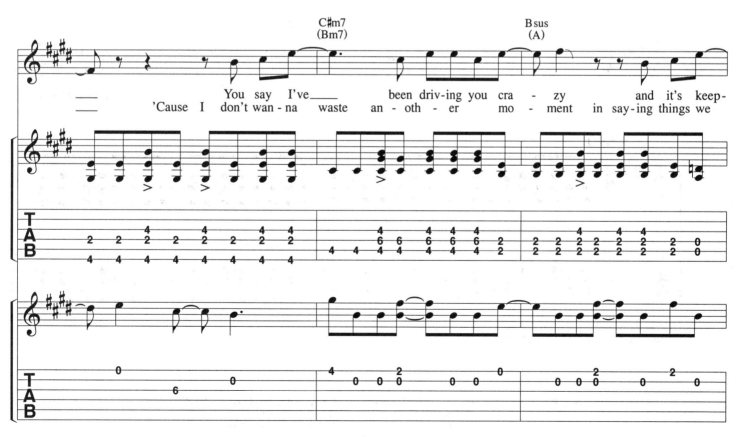

C#m7
(Bm7)

Bsus
(A)

___ You say I've___ been driv-ing you cra - zy___ and it's keep-
___ 'Cause I don't wan - na waste an - oth - er mo - ment in say-ing things we

12

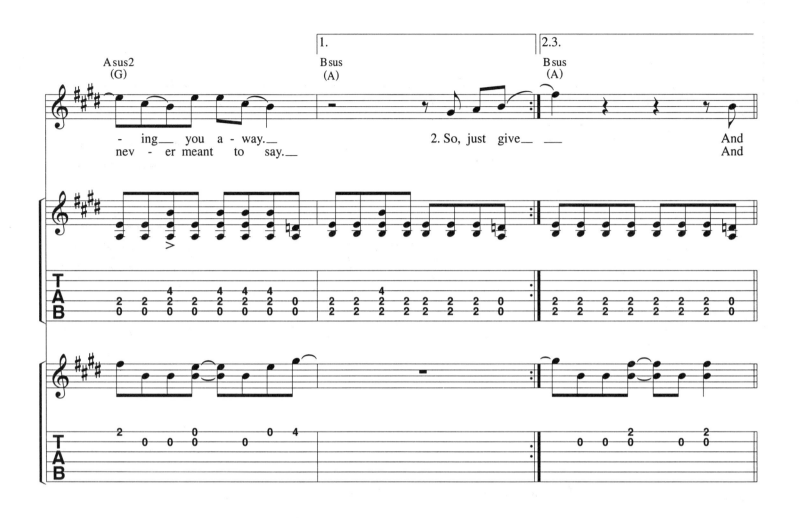

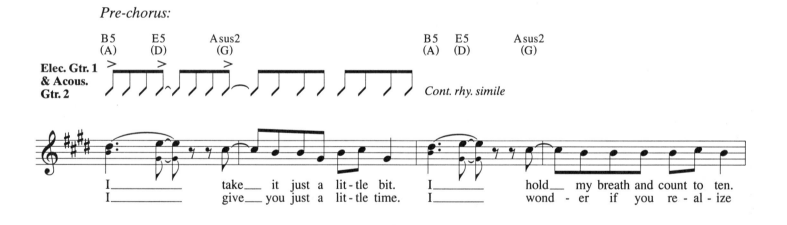

Pre-chorus:

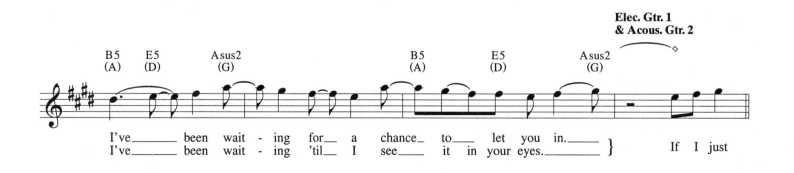

Breathe - 6 - 3

14

Outro Chorus:

w/Rhy. Fig. 1 *(Elec. Gtr. 1)* **& 1A** *(Elec. Gtr. 2) 2 times, simile*

A5 B5 C#5 A5 E5 E/G# B5

breathe___ let___ it fill the space be - tween. I'll know ev - 'ry-thing is al - right.___
Bkgd. Vcl.: Breathe.
yeah, yeah.
Bkgd. Vcl.: Ev - 'ry-thing is al - right.___

1.

A5 B5 C#5 A5 E5 E/G# B5

___ Breathe,___ ev - 'ry lit-tle piece of me, you'll see, ev - 'ry-thing is al - right.___
___ Ev-'ry-thing is al - right if I just breathe, breathe.___
Breathe.

2.

w/Rhy. Figs. 1 *(Elec. Gtr. 1)* **& 1A** *(Elec. Gtr. 2) 1st 2 bars, simile*

B5 A5 B5 C#5 A5

___ I've been driv - ing for___ an hour,_____ just___ talk-

E5 Asus2

- ing to___ the rain._____

Elec. Gtr. 2

Verse 3:
Well, it's all so overrated
In not saying how you feel.
So you end up watching chances fade
And wondering what's real.
And I give you just a little time.
(To Pre-chorus:)

BRING ME TO LIFE

Written by Ben Moody,
Amy Lee and David Hodges

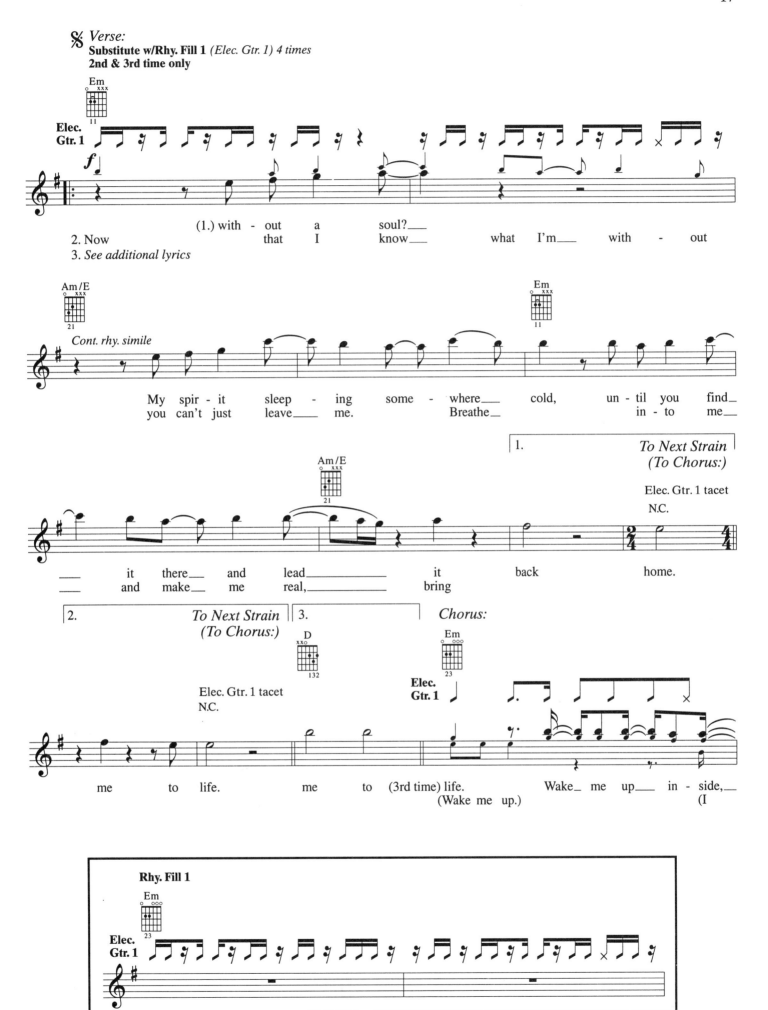

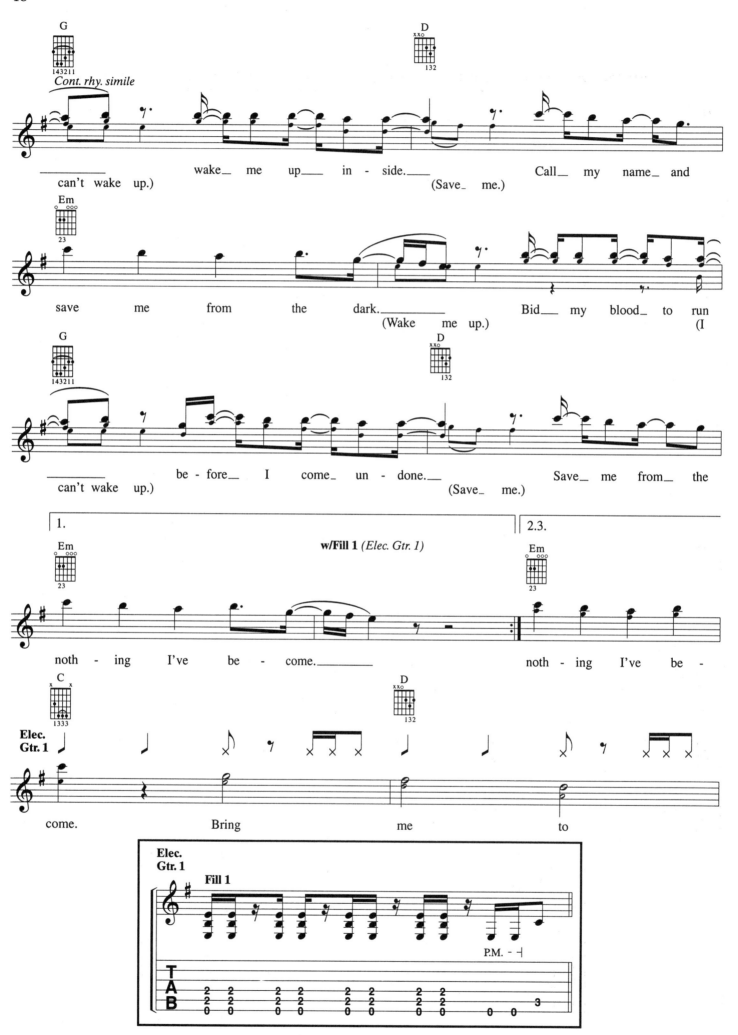

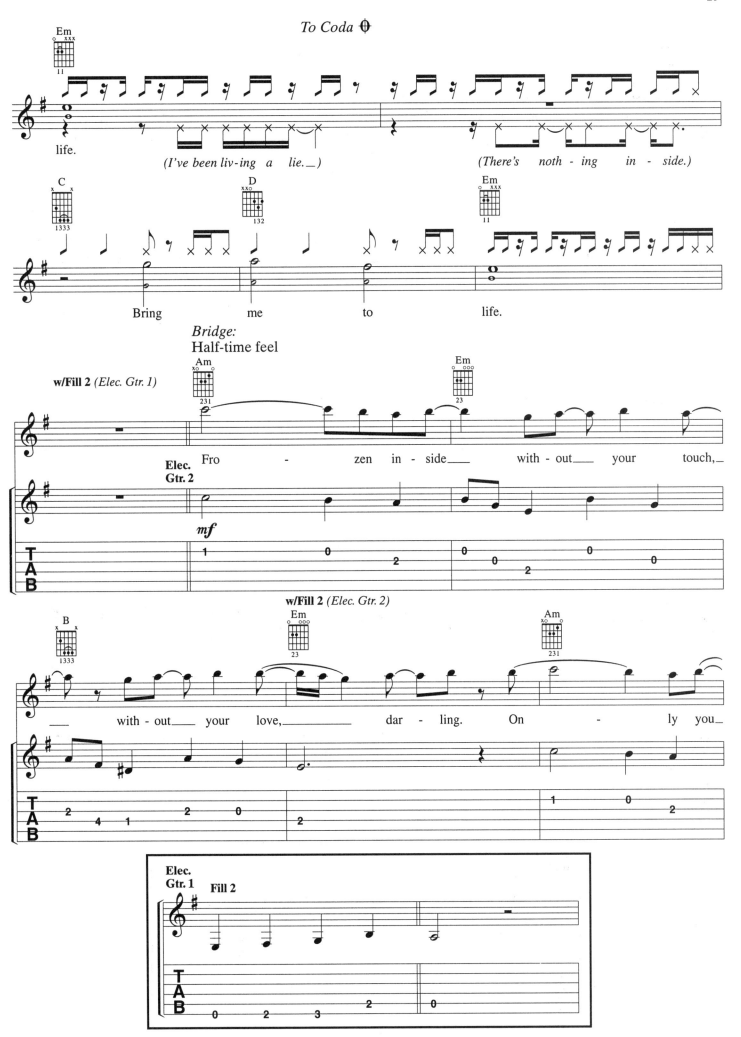

20

Verse 3:
All this time I can't believe I couldn't see.
Kept in the dark, but you were there in front of me.
I've been sleeping a thousand years, it seems.
Got to open my eyes to everything.
Without a thought, without a voice, without a soul,
Don't let me die here.
There must be something more.
Bring me to life.
(To Chorus:)

CLOSURE

*All gtrs. in Drop D, down 1 1/2 steps:

⑥ = B ③ = E
⑤ = F# ② = G#
④ = B ① = C#

D5 F5 G5 A5 Dm B♭sus2

Words by PETE LOEFFLER
Music by CHEVELLE

Moderately fast ♩. = 50

N.C.

Rhy. Fig. 1

Elec. Gtr. 1 *(clean-tone) dbld.*

end Rhy. Fig. 1

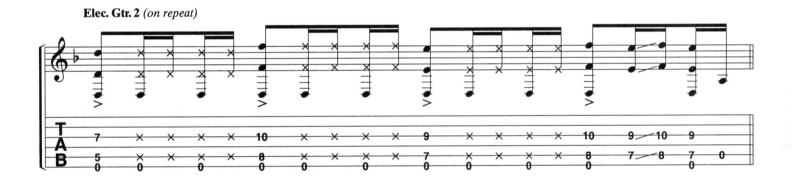

mf hold throughout

*Music sounds a min. 3rd lower than written.

Elec. Gtr. 2 *(on repeat)*

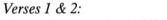

Verses 1 & 2:

w/Rhy. Fig. 1 *(Elec. Gtr. 1, dbld.) 4 times, simile*

D5

1. Breathe, trust, bless me and re - lease, climb hard or nev - er be
turn and lay down your sting of dis - ease phase you out, should-'ve seen this com -

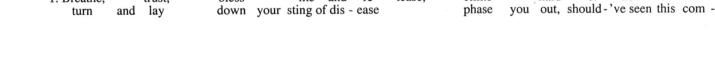

seen. Closed off, res - cue to breathe, just bless me.
ing. Go on con - fus - ing this soul, hold my breath -'til you rup - ture.

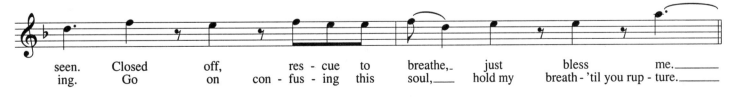

Closure - 5 - 1

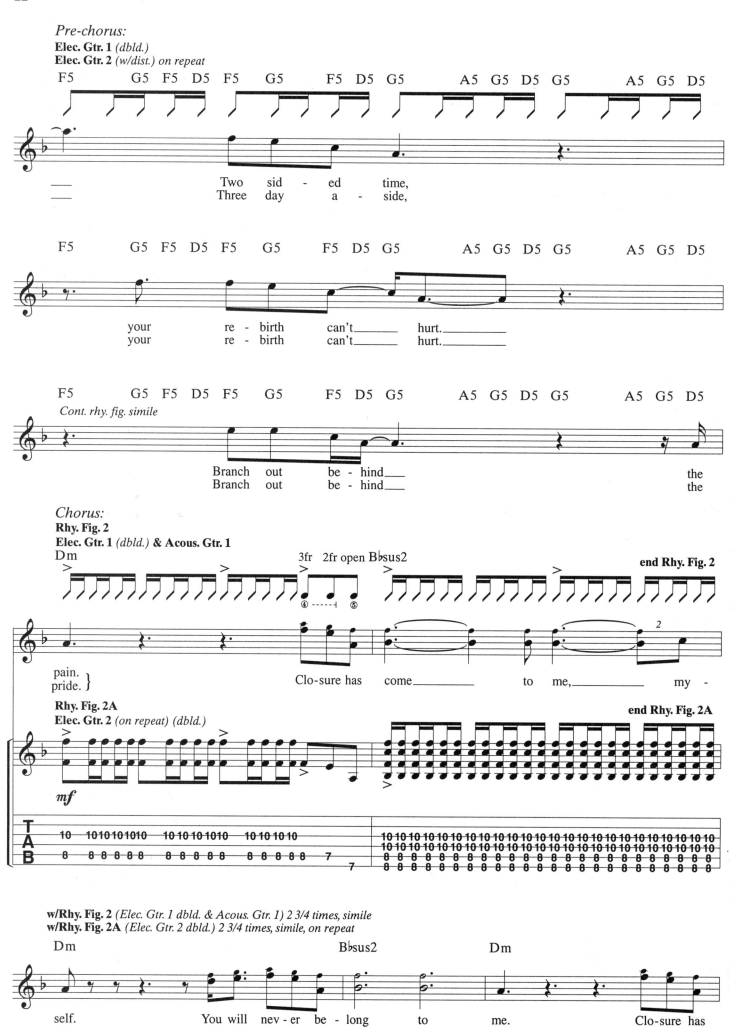

come _____ to me, _____ my - self.   You willl nev - er be -

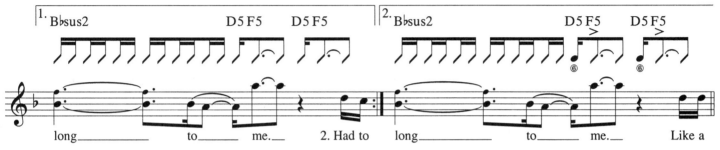

long _____ to _____ me. 2. Had to long _____ to _____ me. _____ Like a

Verse 3:
D5
Cont. in notation

leech, _____ I hold on as if we be - longed _____

Elec. Gtr. 2

_____ to some pre - cious pure dream cast off, you've seen what's be - neath, _____

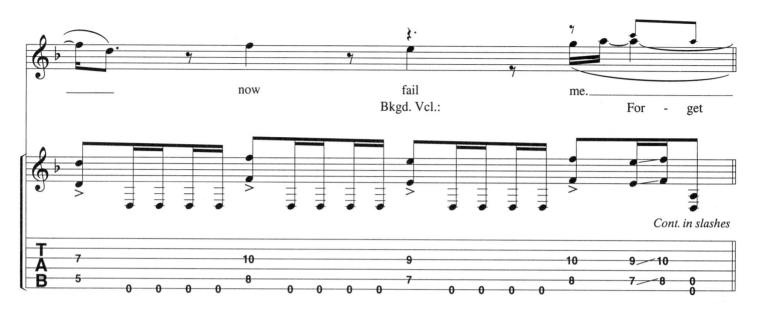

now   fail   me.   For - get

Bkgd. Vcl.:

Cont. in slashes

Pre-chorus:

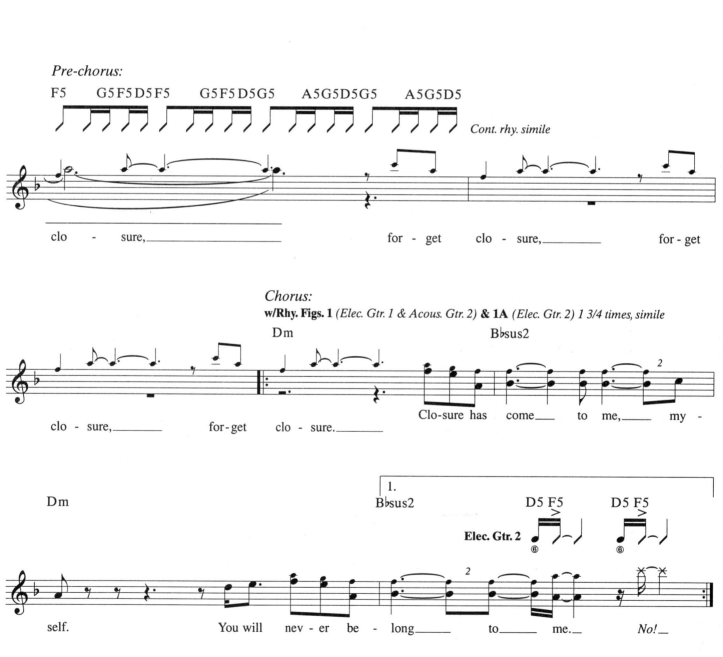

F5   G5 F5 D5 F5   G5 F5 D5 G5   A5 G5 D5 G5   A5 G5 D5

Cont. rhy. simile

clo - sure,   for - get   clo - sure,   for - get

Chorus:

w/Rhy. Figs. 1 *(Elec. Gtr. 1 & Acous. Gtr. 2)* **& 1A** *(Elec. Gtr. 2) 1 3/4 times, simile*

Dm   B♭sus2

clo - sure,   for-get   clo - sure.   Clo-sure has   come   to   me,   my -

Dm   B♭sus2   D5 F5   D5 F5

1.

Elec. Gtr. 2

self.   You will   nev - er be - long   to   me.   *No!*

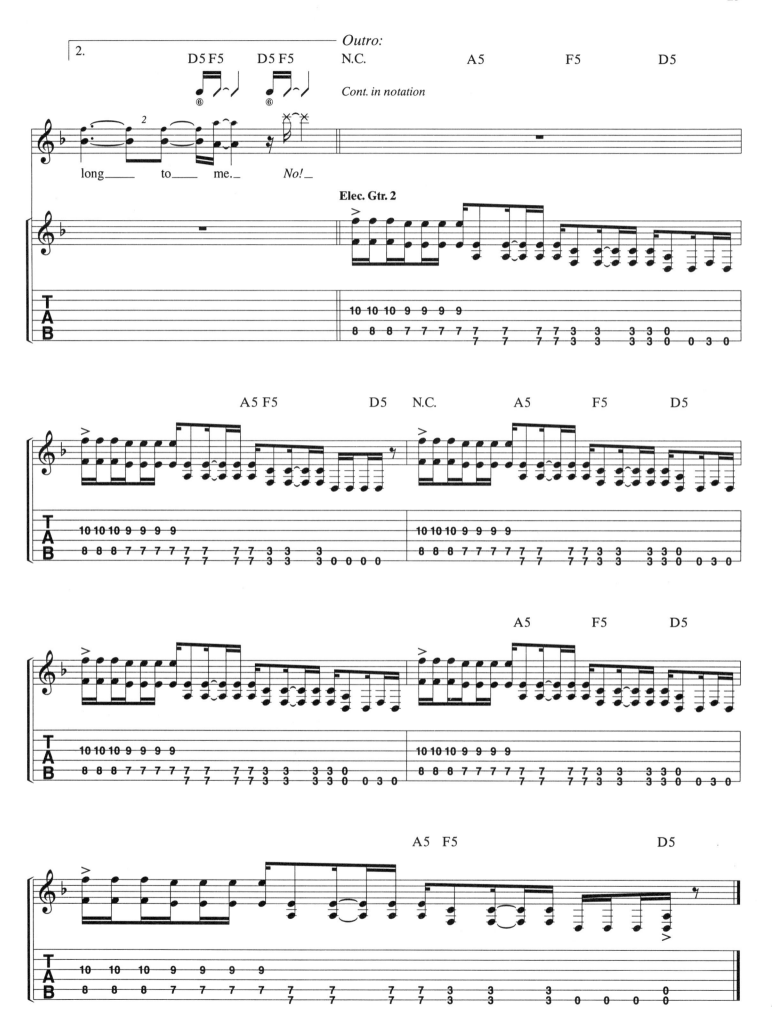

All gtrs. are 7-string gtrs.
tuned down 1 whole step:

⑦ = A   ③ = F
⑥ = D   ② = A
⑤ = G   ① = D
④ = C

DID MY TIME

Words and Music by
JONATHAN DAVIS,
JAMES SHAFFER, BRIAN WELCH,
REGINALD ARVIZU and DAVID SILVERIA

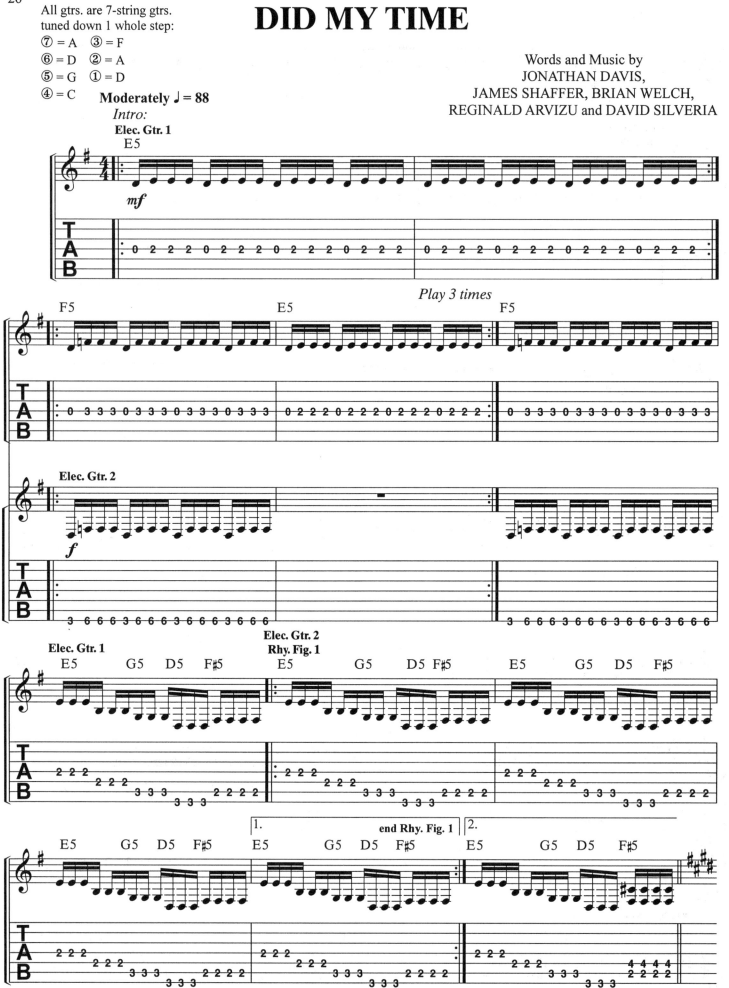

DRIVEN UNDER

Words and Music by
SHAUN WELGEMOED

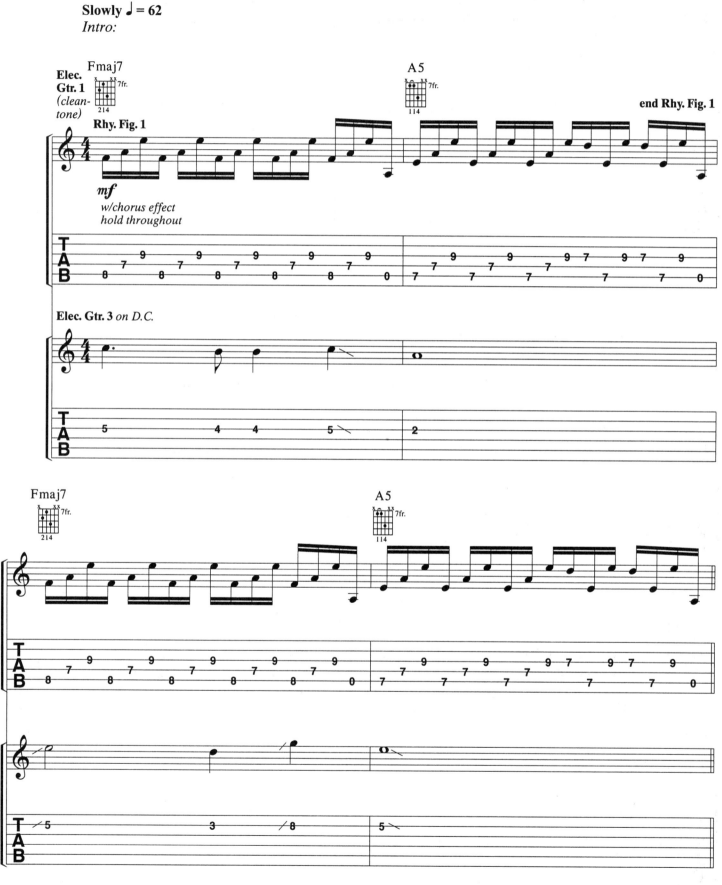

Driven Under - 5 - 2

Verse 3:
I guess you know I'm faking
When I tell you I love you.
Guess you know that I am blind
To everything you say and do.
Must be something on my mind.
There's nothing left for me to hide.
Do you know I'm faking?
(To Chorus:)

FAINT

All gtrs. in Drop D, down 1/2 step:

⑥ = C♯   ③ = F♯
⑤ = G♯   ② = A♯
④ = C♯   ① = D♯

By LINKIN PARK

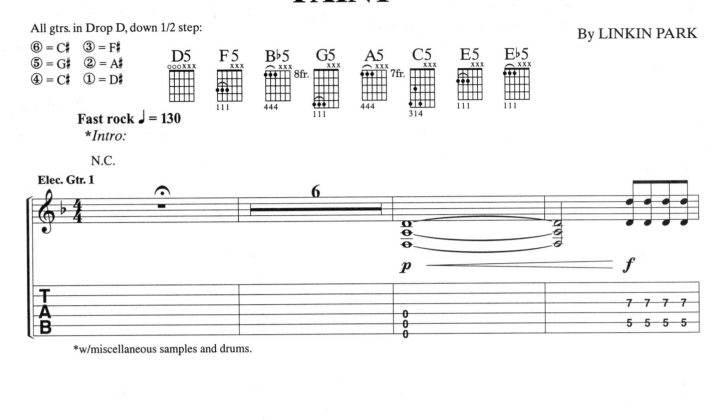

Fast rock ♩ = 130
Intro:

*w/miscellaneous samples and drums.

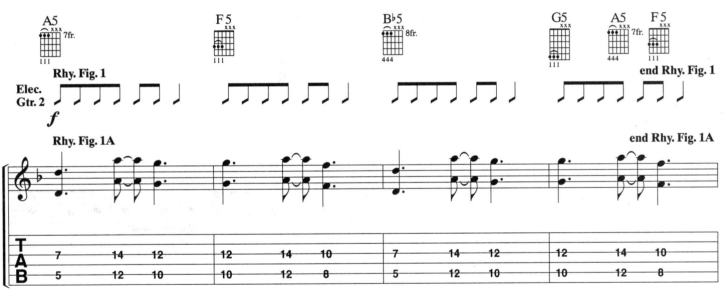

Elec. Gtrs. 1 & 2 cont. simile

Elec. Gtr. 1 tacet

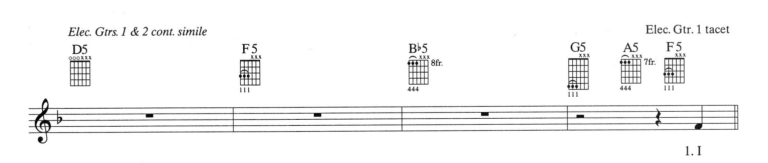

1. I

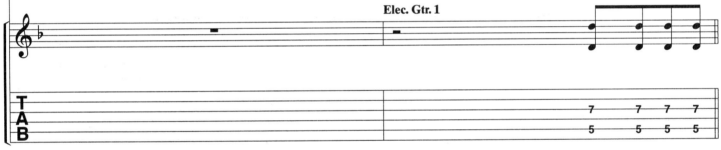

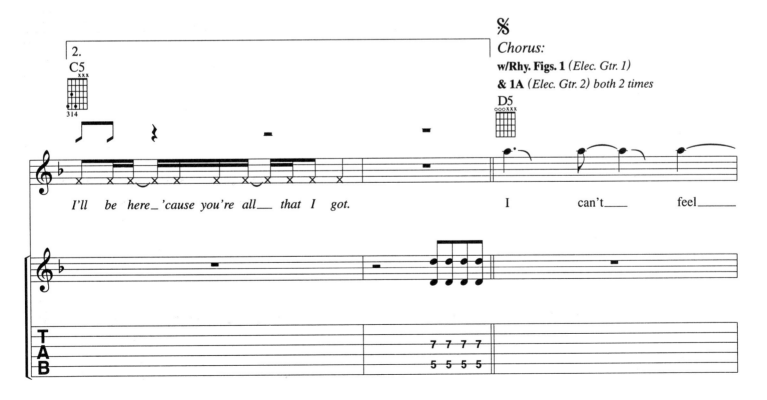

Faint - 5 - 3

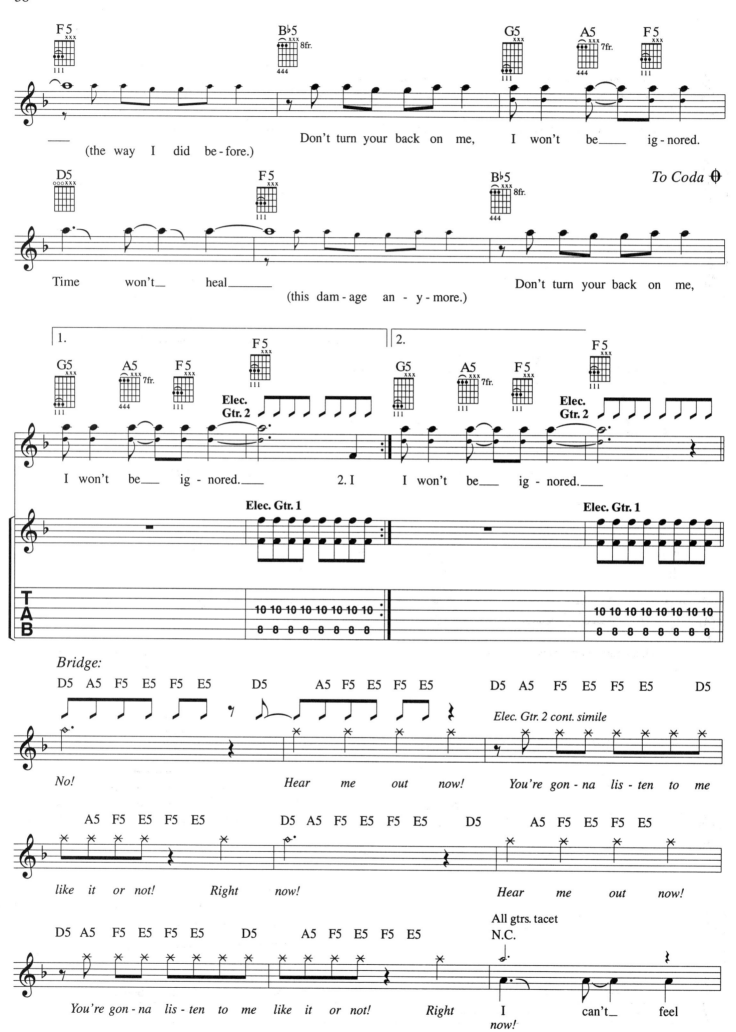

D.S. 𝄋 al Coda

the way I did be-fore.   Don't turn your back on me,   *I won't be___ ig - nored._____*

w/fdbk.

p < *f*

(7)

w/Rhy. Figs. 1 *(Elec. Gtr. 1)* & 1A *(Elec. Gtr. 2) both 2 times*

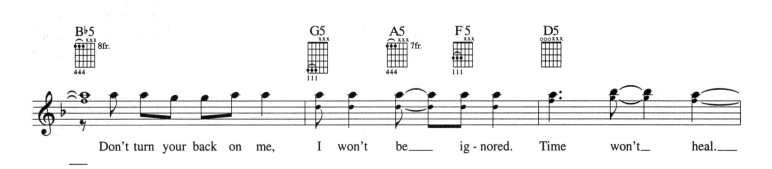

Coda

I won't be___ ig - nored.   I   can't___   feel._____

Don't turn your back on me,   I won't be___ ig - nored.   Time   won't___   heal.___

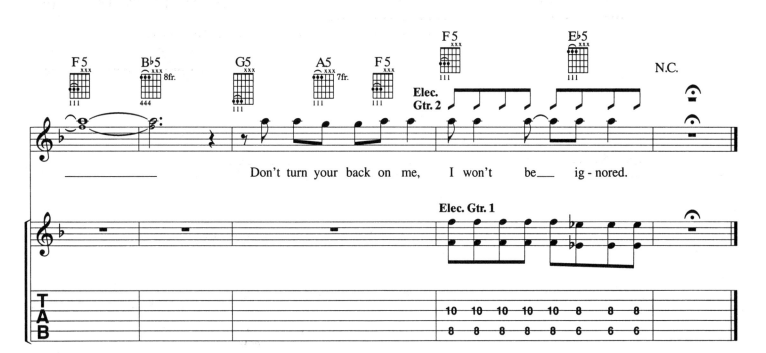

_____   Don't turn your back on me,   I won't   be___ ig - nored.

Elec. Gtr. 2

Elec. Gtr. 1

N.C.

FIGURED YOU OUT

Lyrics by
CHAD KROEGER
Music by
NICKELBACK

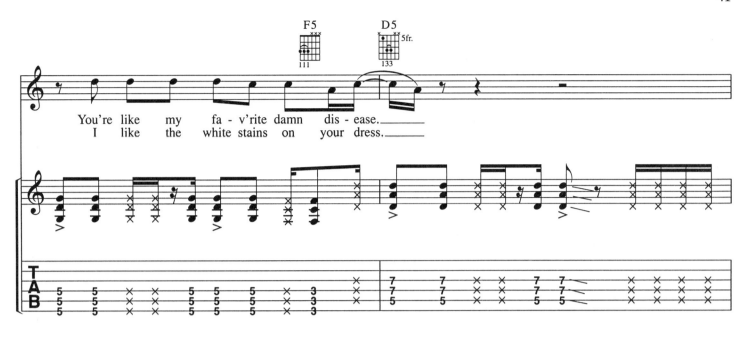

You're like my fa-v'rite damn dis-ease._____
I like the white stains on your dress._____

Gtrs. re-enter on D.S.

And I {1. love / 3. hate} the plac-es that__ we go_____
And I love the way__ you pass__ the check__

Elec. Gtr. 2 *(w/dist.)*

mf

Elec. Gtr. 1

w/A.H. throughout

harm. - - - - - - - - 4   harm. - - - - - - - - - 4

Figured You Out - 7 - 2

42

44

To Coda

Interlude:

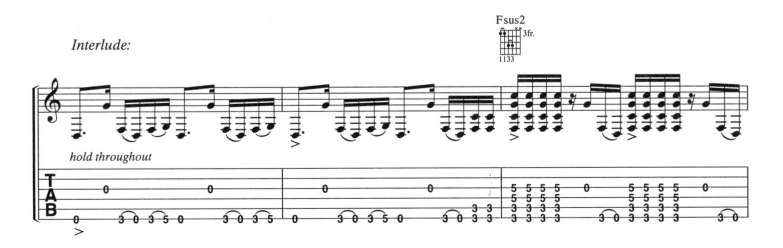

3.I like your pants_ a - round_ your feet_

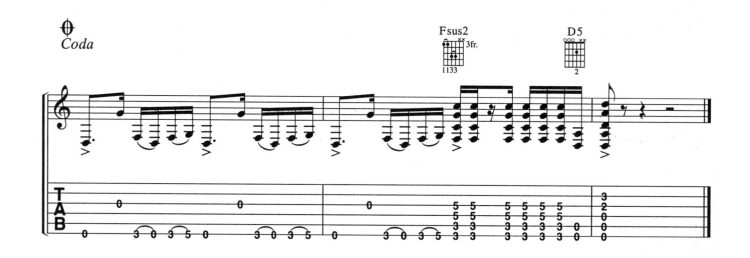

THE GAME OF LOVE

Words and Music by
ALEX ANDER and RICK NOWELS

*Composite arrangement.

The Game of Love - 11 - 1

48

Guitar Solo:

54

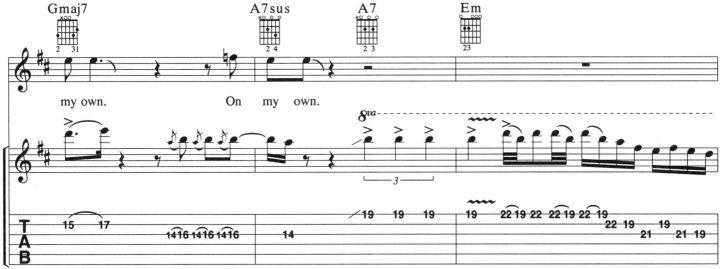

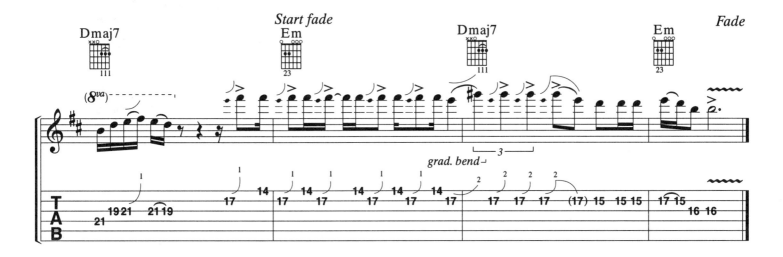

GOING UNDER

60

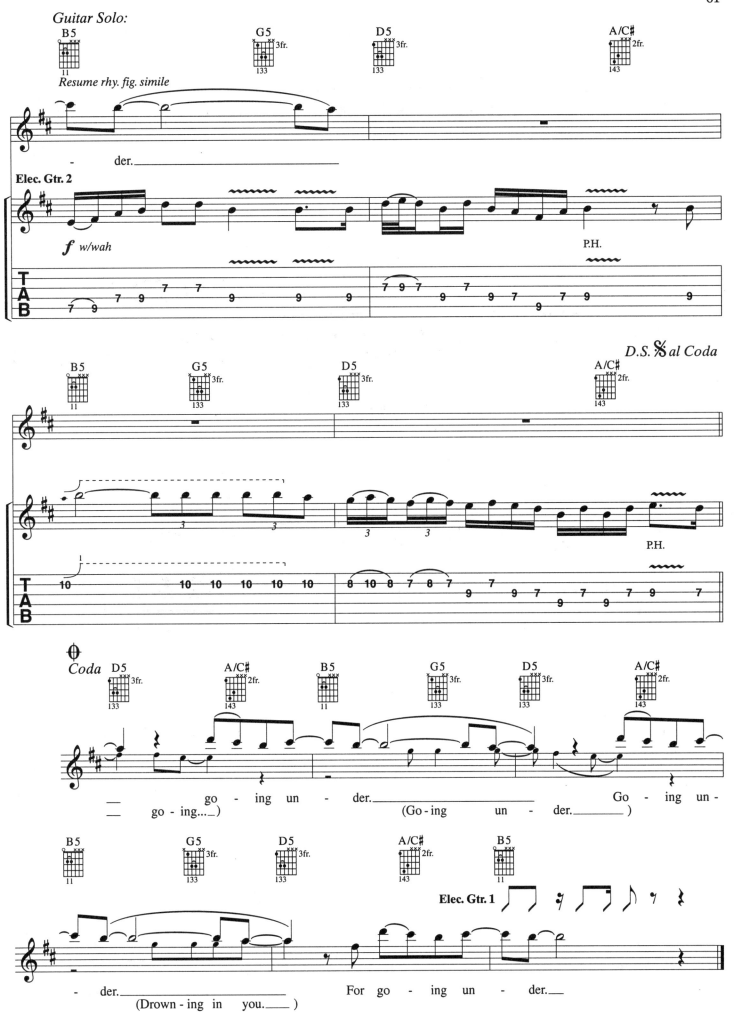

HEAD ON COLLISION

Words and Music by
JORDAN I. PUNDIK, IAN R. GRUSHKA,
CHAD EVERETT GILBERT,
CYRUS WILLIAM BOLOOKI and STEPHEN LEE KLEIN

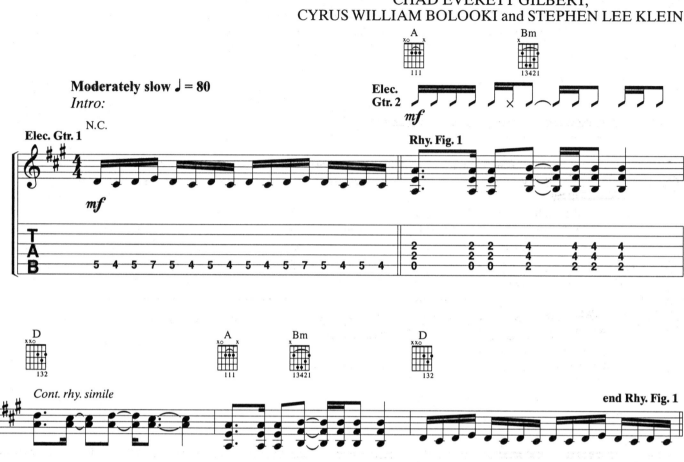

64

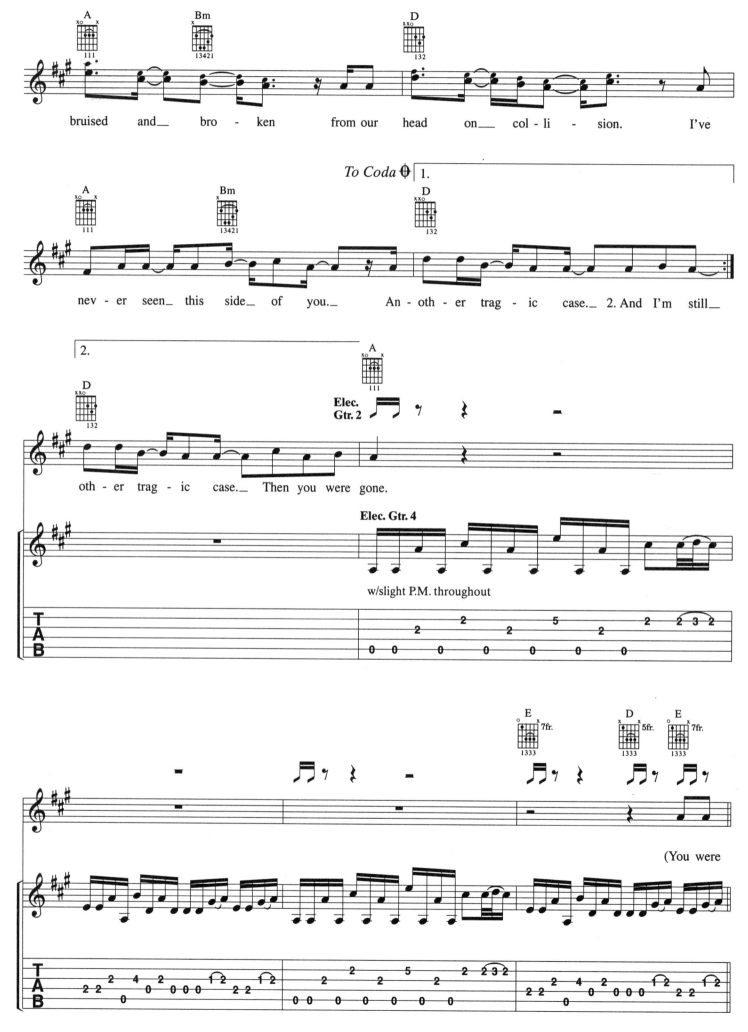

66

-er trag - ic case___ a night - mare.___ (Still wait - ing for a good day.___)

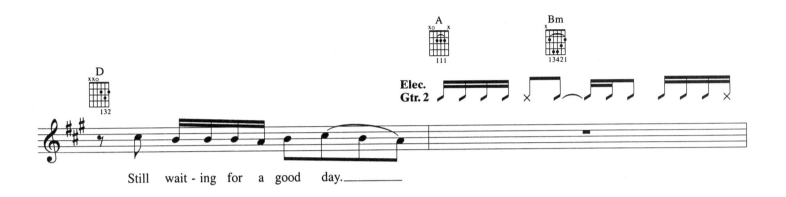

Still wait - ing for a good day.___

HEADSTRONG

Music by
CHRIS BROWN, PETER CHARELL
and SIMON ORMANDY
Lyrics by
CHRIS BROWN

Moderate rock ♩ = 92
Intro:

*Tune 7th string to B.

Headstrong - 7 - 1

Double-time feel
w/Riff A *(6-string Gtr. 1)*
7-string Gtr. tacet

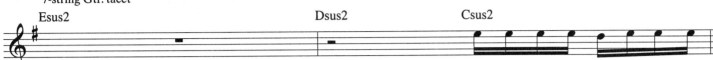

1. Cir - cl - ing, you're cir - cl - ing, you're

Verse:
w/Riff A *(6-string Gtr. 1) 4 times*

cir - cl - ing your head,   con - tem - plat - ing   ev - 'ry - thing you ev - er said.   Now   I   see the
clu - sions man - i - fest your first im - pres - sion's got to   be your ver - y best.   I see you're full of

end Double-time feel

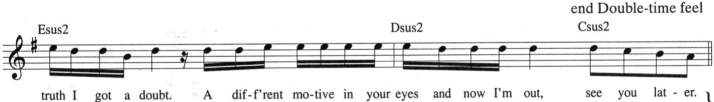

truth I   got a doubt.   A   dif - f'rent mo - tive in   your eyes   and now I'm out,   see you lat - er.
shit and that's al - right.   That's how you play, I guess, you get through ev - 'ry night. Well, now that's o - ver.

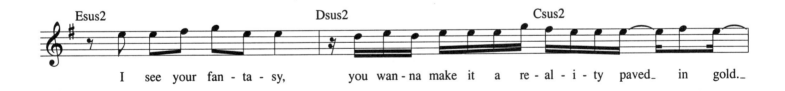

___ See in - side, in - side of our heads, yeah.   Well, now that's o - ver,   I see your

Headstrong - 7 - 2

72

*On repeats play 12th fret harm.
on 5th string.

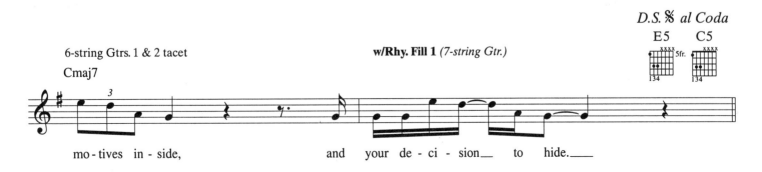

NOT FALLING

Words and Music by
MATTHEW McDONOUGH, GREG TRIBBETT,
RYAN MARTINIE and CHAD GRAY

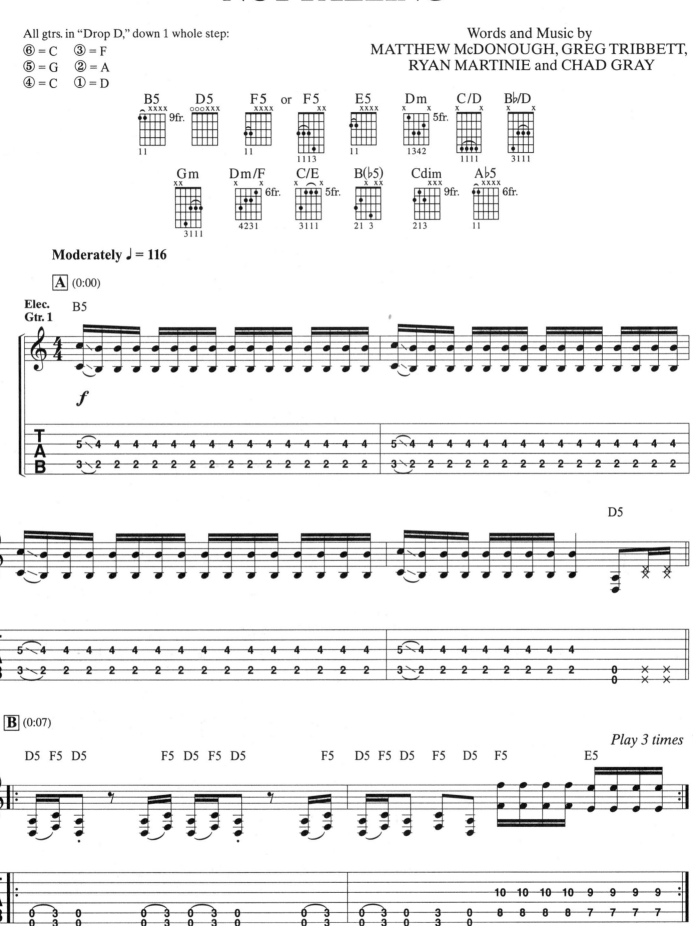

Not Falling - 13 - 1

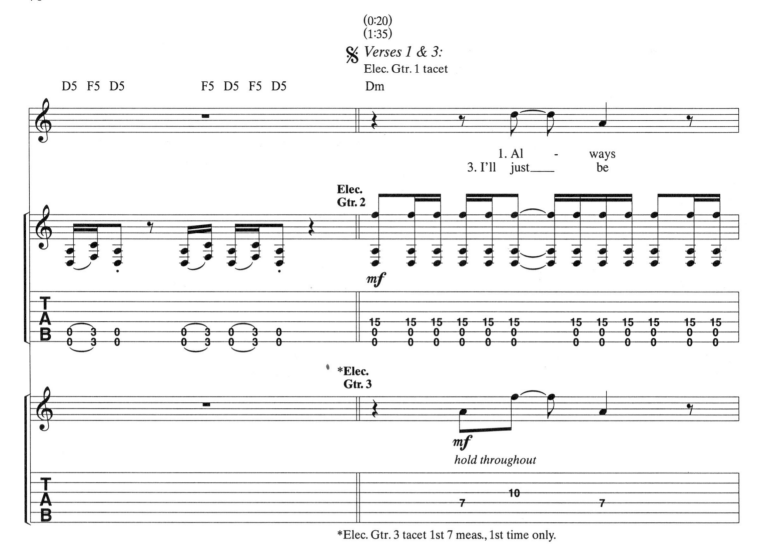

*Elec. Gtr. 3 tacet 1st 7 meas., 1st time only.

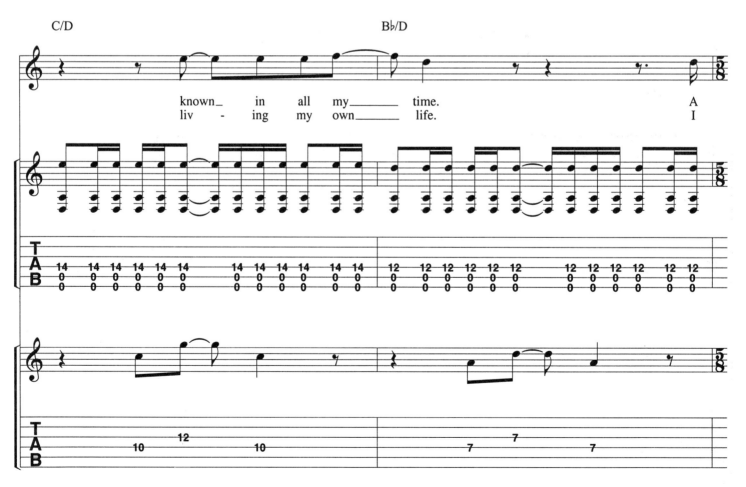

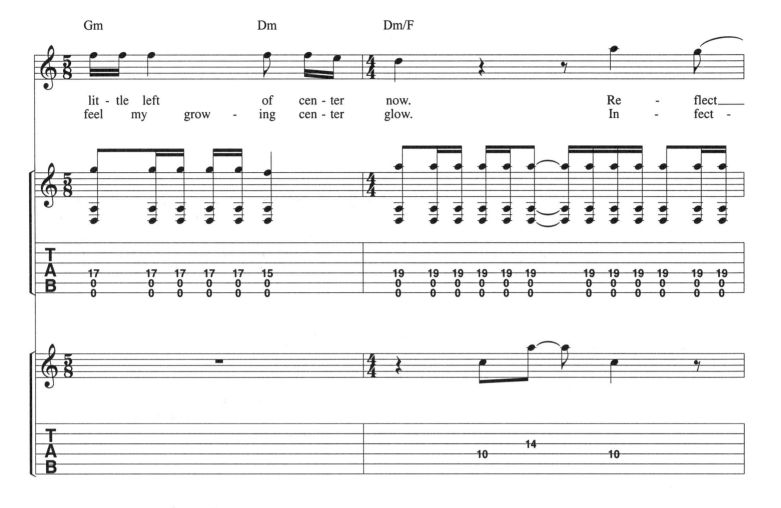

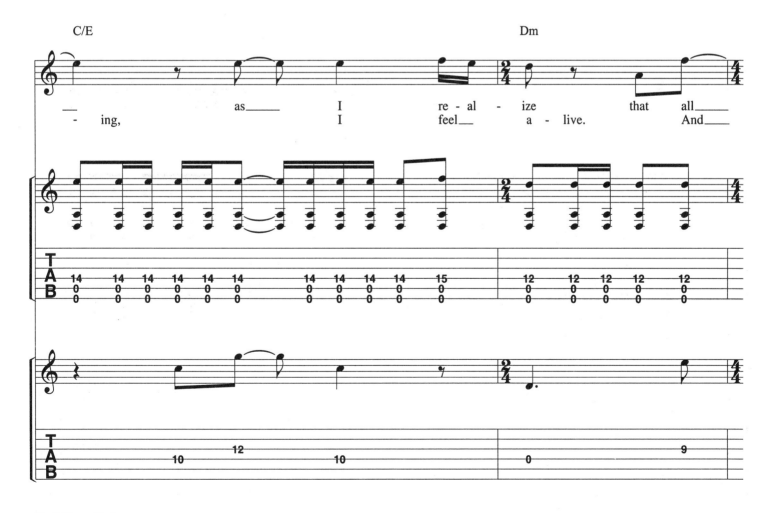

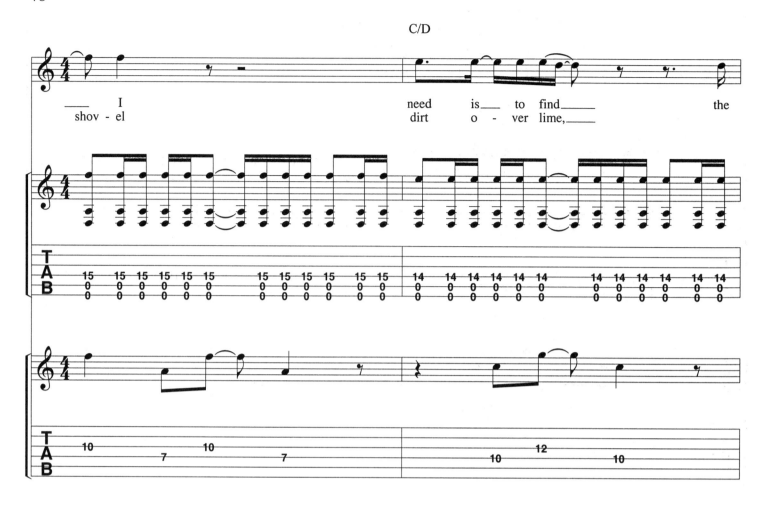

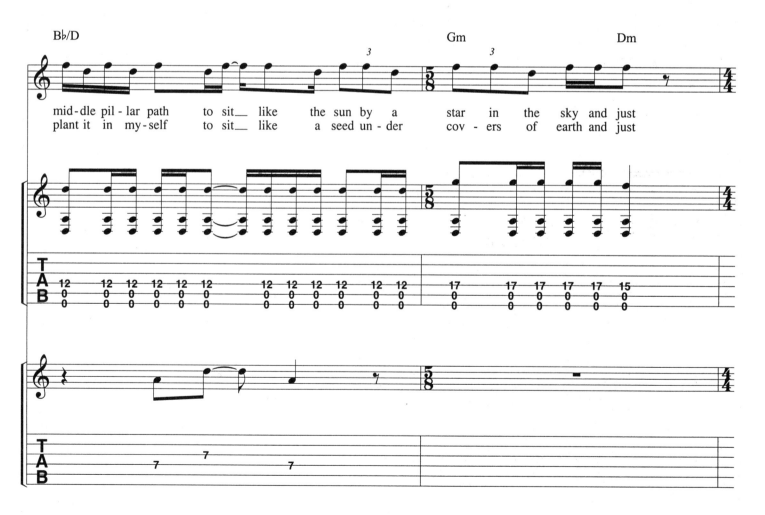

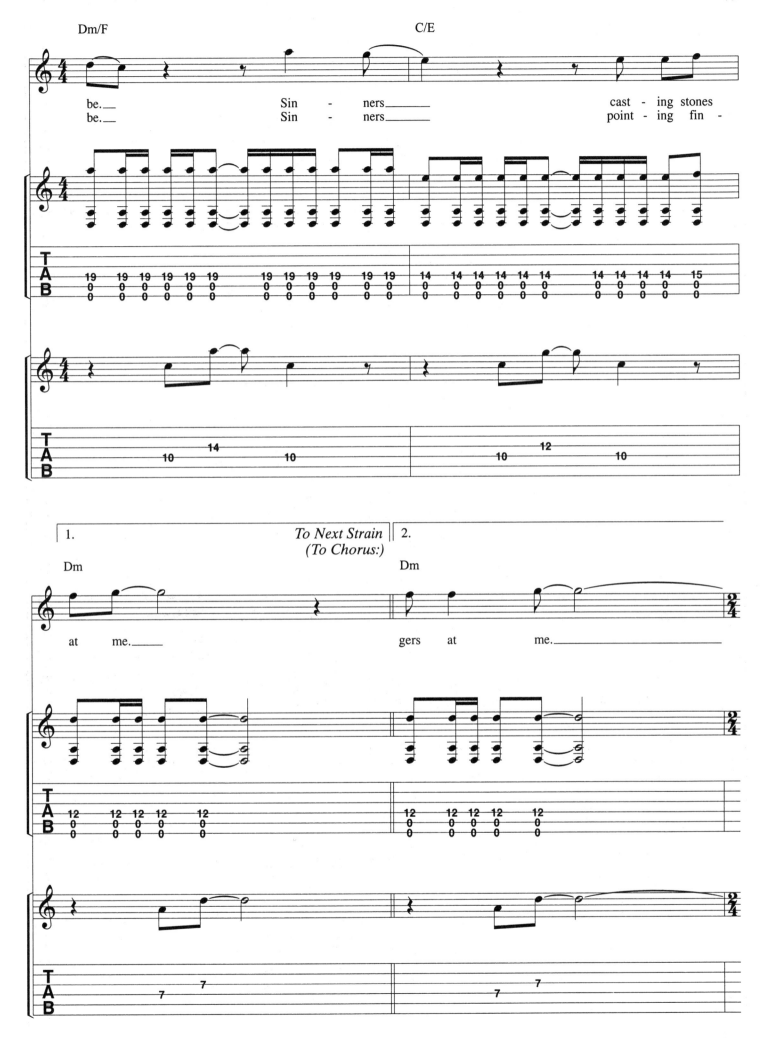

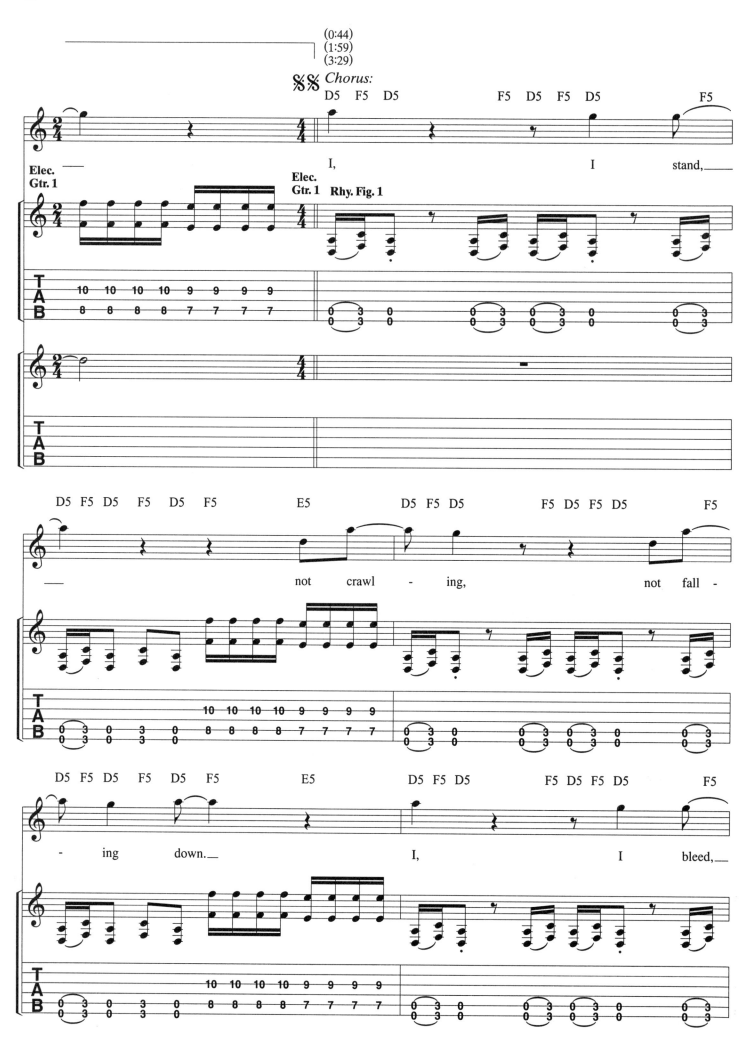

84

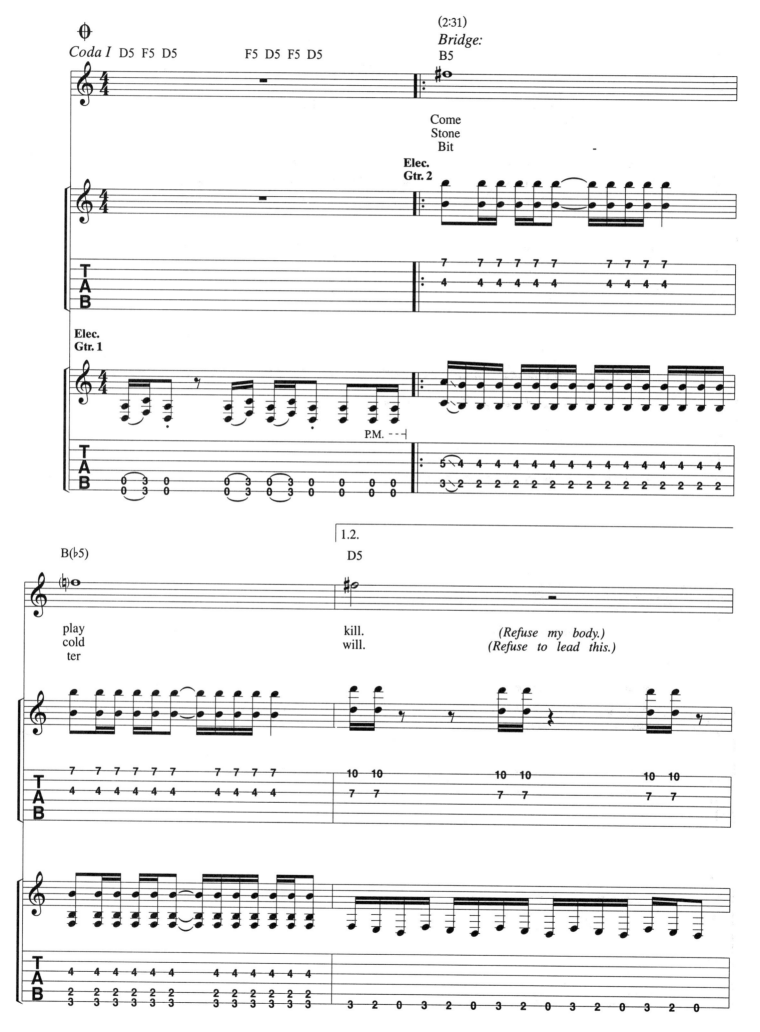

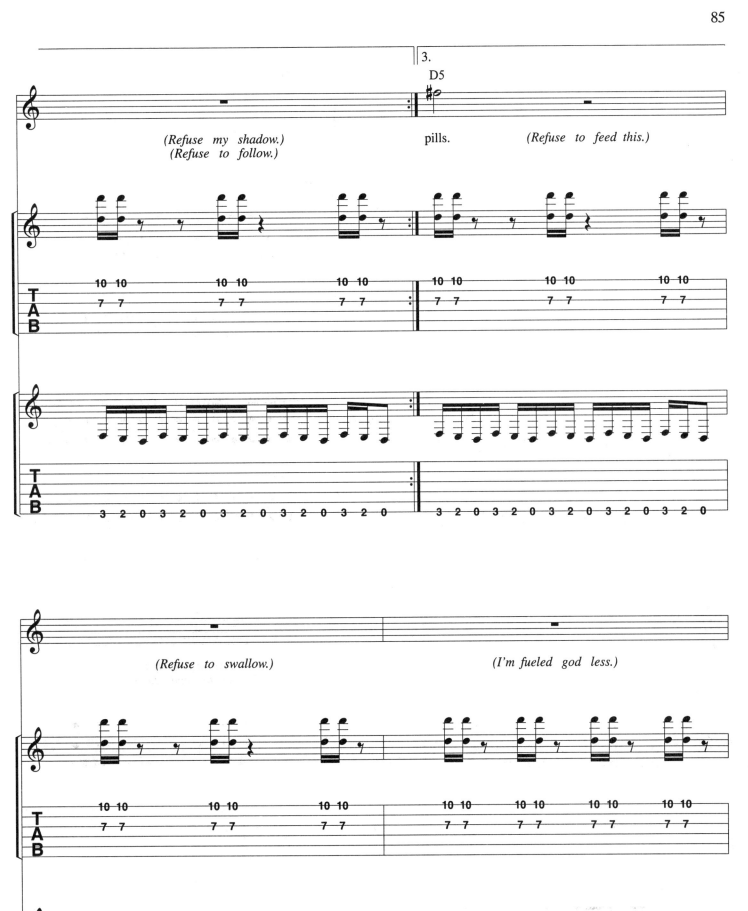

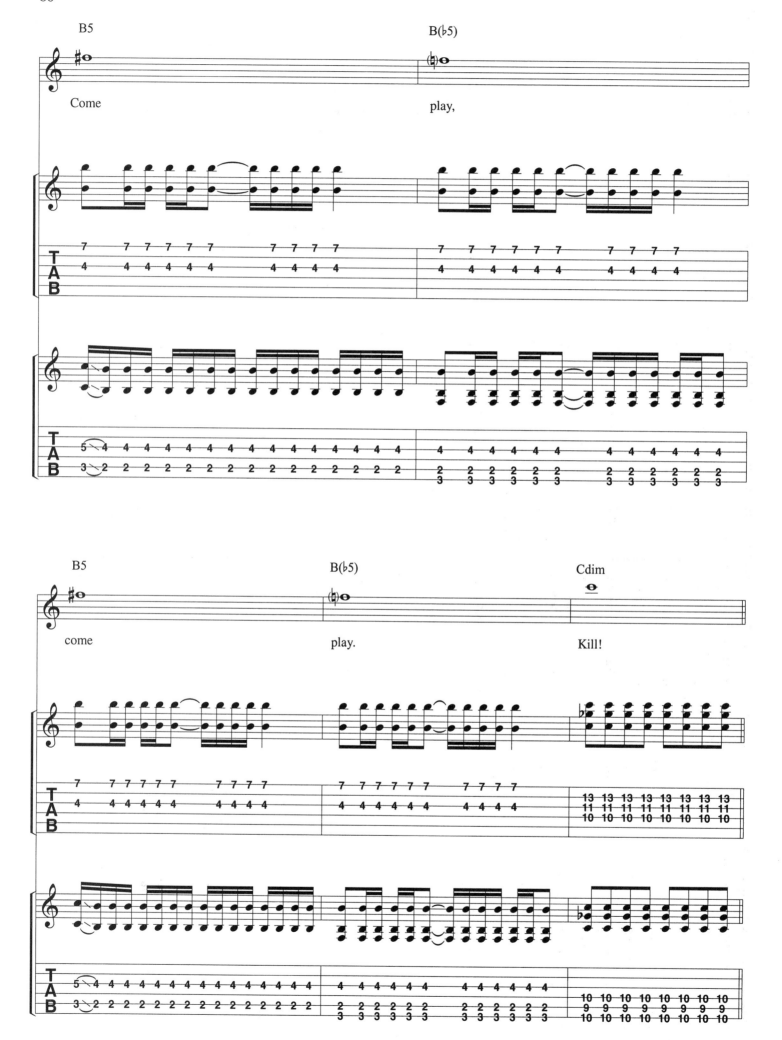

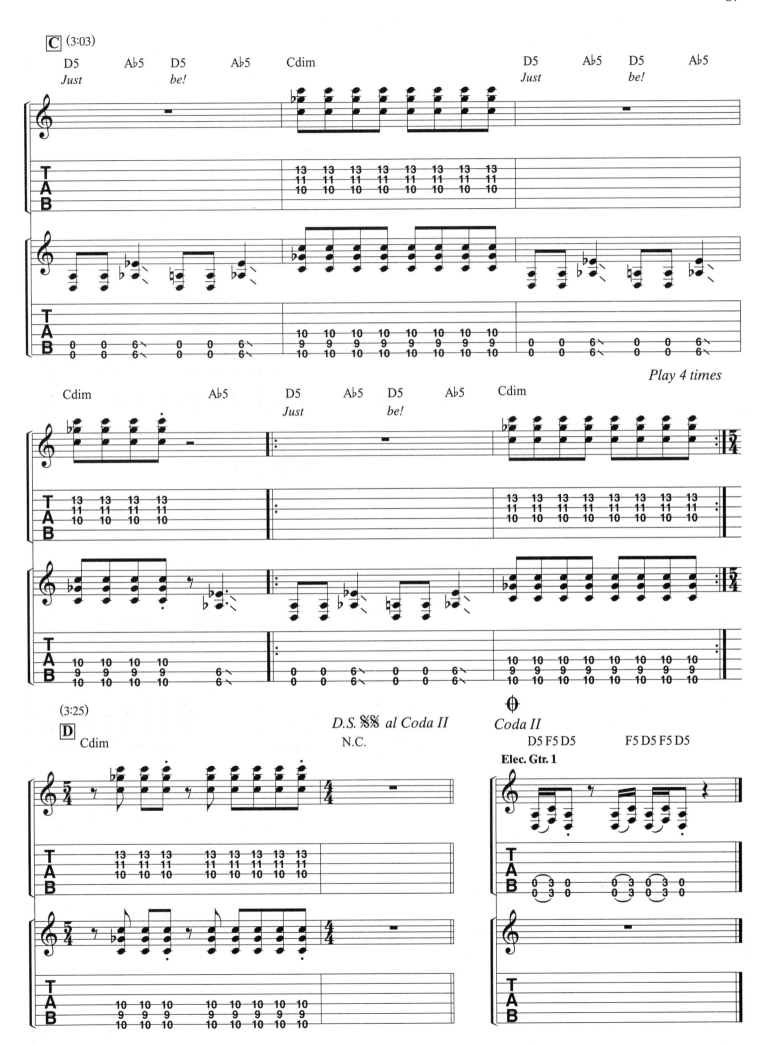

HERE WITHOUT YOU

Tune down 1/2 step:

⑥ = E♭ ③ = G♭
⑤ = A♭ ② = B♭
④ = D♭ ① = E♭

Words and Music by
**BRAD ARNOLD, ROBERT TODD HARRELL,
CHRISTOPHER LEE HENDERSON
and MATTHEW DARRICK ROBERTS**

days have made me old-er___ since the last___ time that___ I saw___ your pret-ty face.___
miles just___ keep roll-in' as the peo-ple leave their way___ to say hel-lo.___

A thou-sand
I've heard this

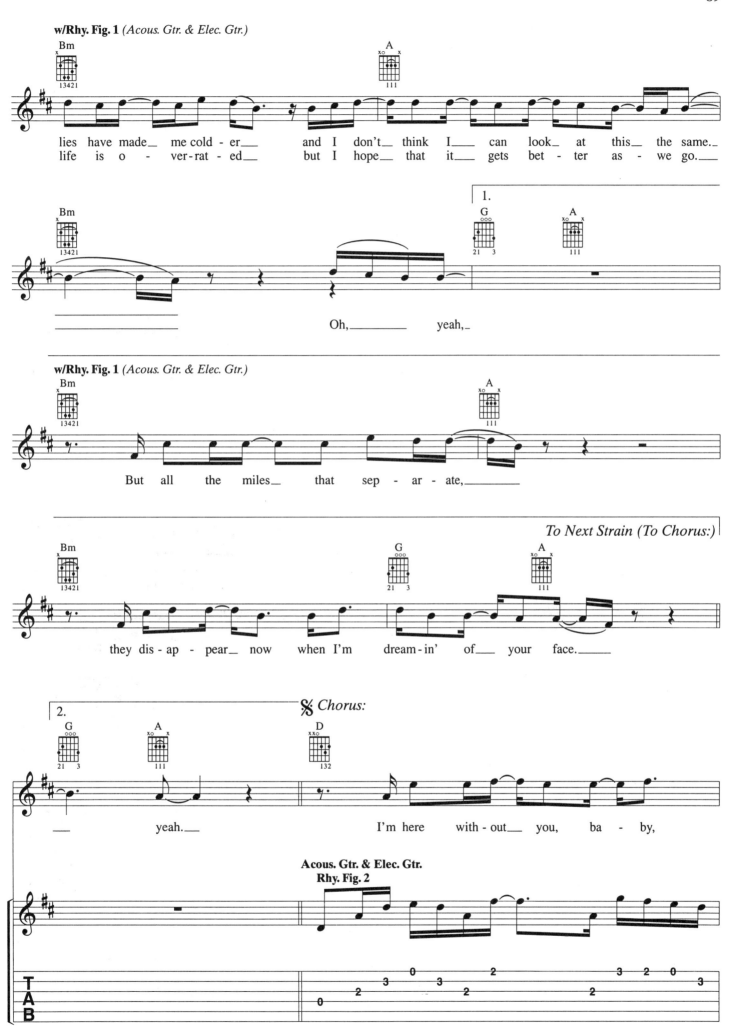

LIBERATE

94

Liberate - 6 - 3

MINERVA

Words and Music by
CAMILLO "CHINO" MORENO,
STEPHEN CARPENTER, CHI CHENG,
ABE CUNNINGHAM and FRANK DELGATO

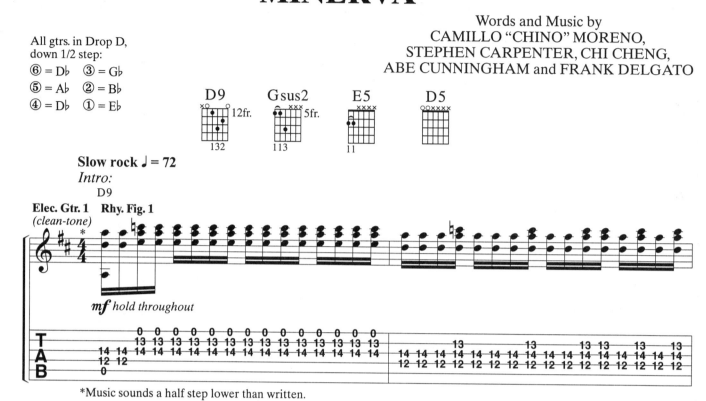

All gtrs. in Drop D,
down 1/2 step:
⑥ = D♭ ③ = G♭
⑤ = A♭ ②= B♭
④ = D♭ ① = E♭

Slow rock ♩ = 72
Intro:

*Music sounds a half step lower than written.

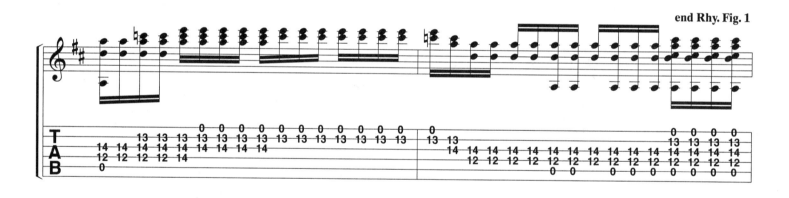

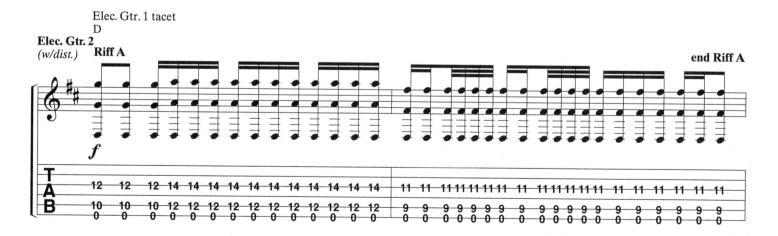

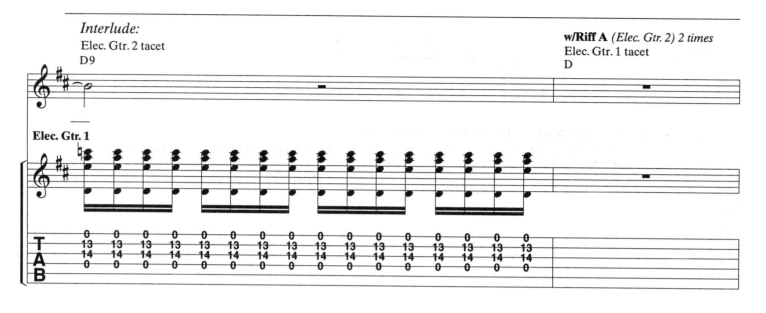

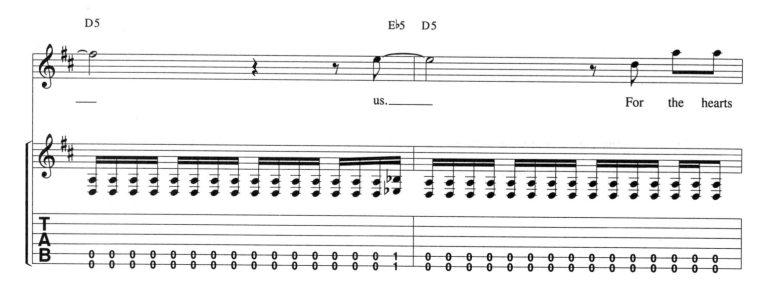

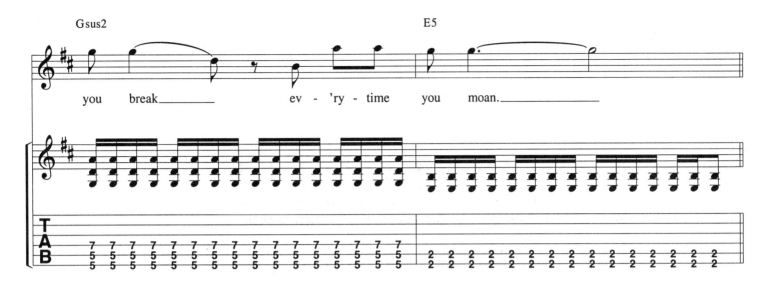

you break_____ ev - 'ry - time you moan._____

Interlude:
w/Rhy. Fig. 1 *(Elec. Gtr. 1)*
Elec. Gtr. 2 tacet

Elec. Gtr. 3 tacet

D.S. % al Coda

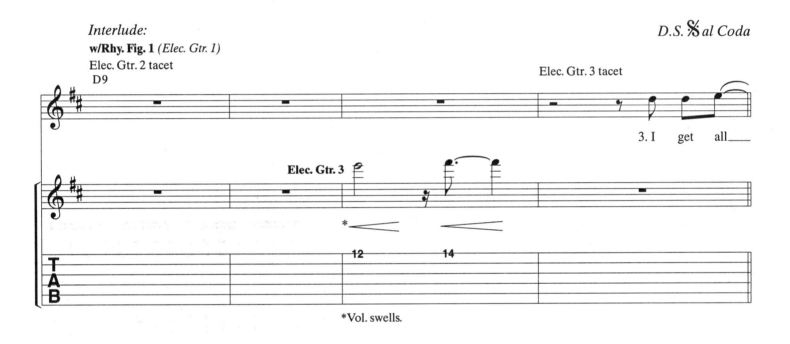

3. I get all___

Elec. Gtr. 3

*Vol. swells.

Coda

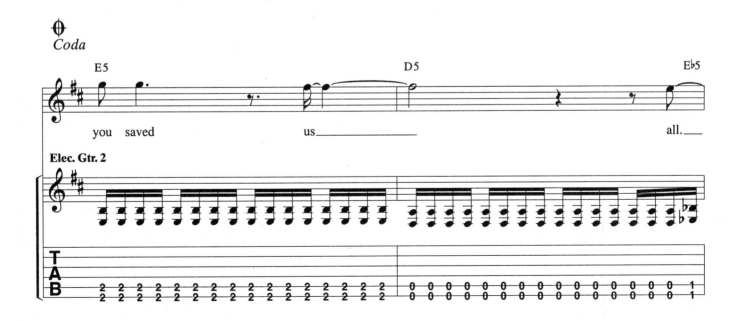

you saved us_____ all.___

Elec. Gtr. 2

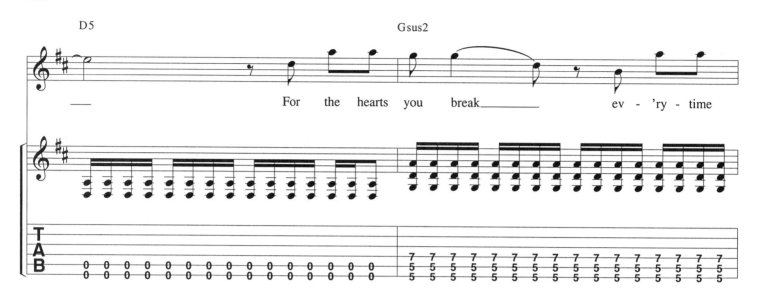

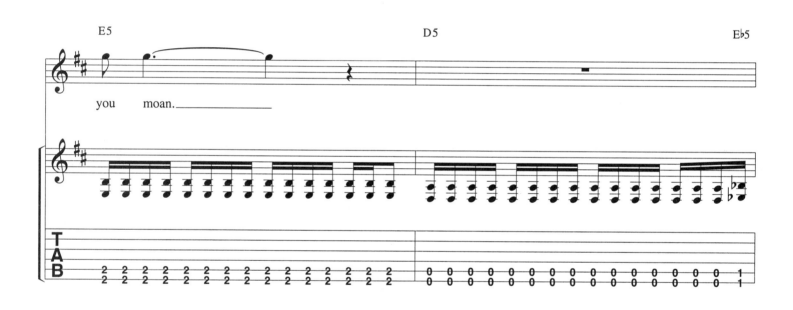

Outro:

Elec. Gtr. 2 tacet

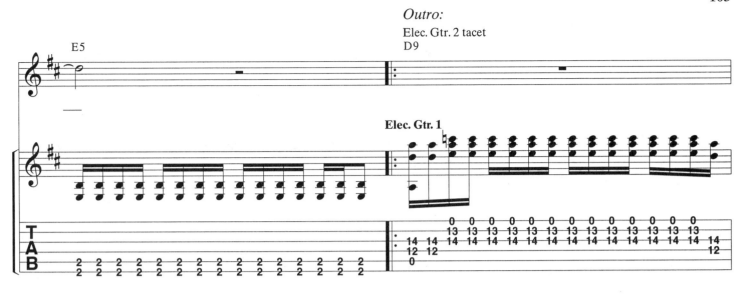

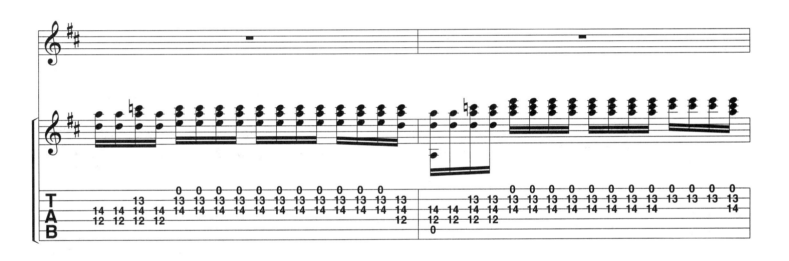

Repeat and fade

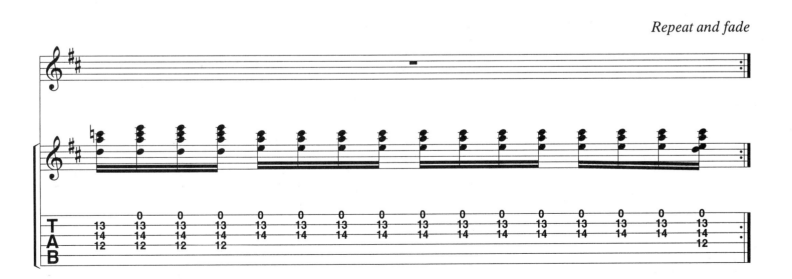

NEVER AGAIN

Lyrics by CHAD KROEGER
Music by NICKELBACK

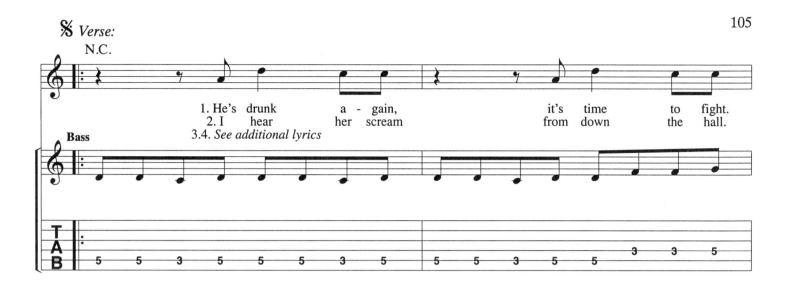

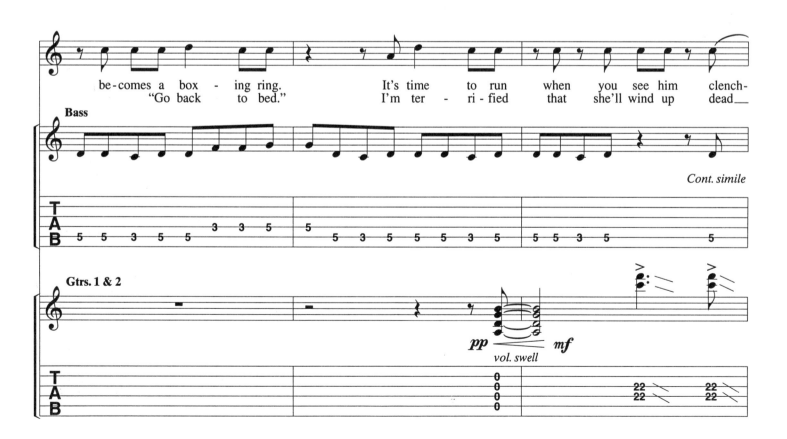

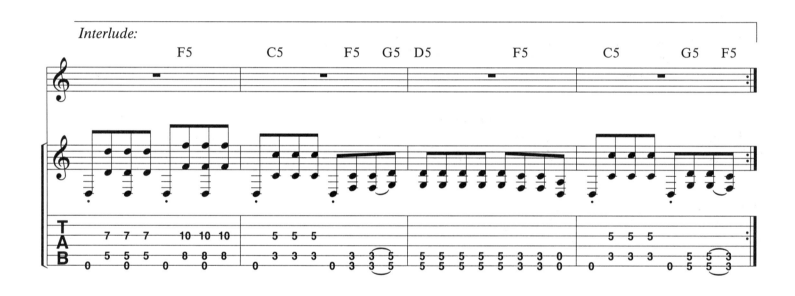

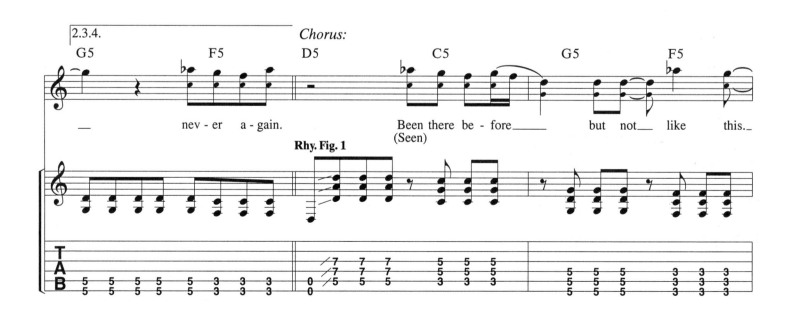

Seen it be-fore____ but not_ like this.____ Nev-er be-fore____ have I__ ev - er
(Been)

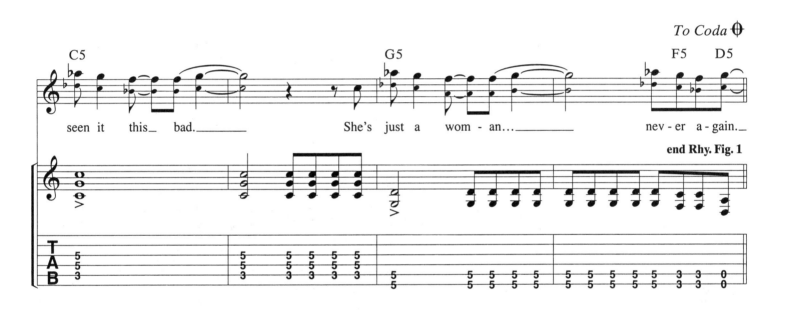

seen it this_ bad.____ She's just a wom - an...____ nev - er a-gain._

To Coda ⊕

end Rhy. Fig. 1

1.
Interlude:

D.S. %

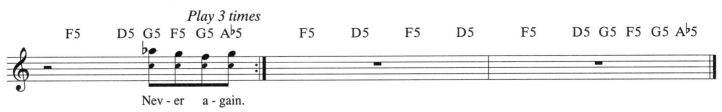

Verse 3:
Just tell the nurse you slipped and fell.
It starts to sting as it starts to swell.
She looks at you… she wants the truth.
It's right out there in the waiting room with those hands
Lookin' just as sweet as he can… never again.
(To Chorus:)

Verse 4:
He's drunk again, it's time to fight.
Same old s***, just on a different night.
She grabs the gun, she's had enough.
Tonight she'll find out how f***in' tough is this man.
Pulls the trigger as fast as she can… never again.
(To Chorus:)

NUMB

By LINKIN PARK

All gtrs. in Drop D, down 1/2 step:

⑥ = C♯ ③ = F♯
⑤ = G♯ ② = A♯
④ = C♯ ① = D♯

Moderately ♩ = 108

Intro:

N.C.

Keybd. 1 *(arr. for gtr.)*

Elec. Gtr. 1

Cont. in slashes

fdbk.

Keybd. 1 cont. simile

G5	E♭5	B♭5/F	F 5

Rhy. Fig. 1 Elec. Gtr. 1

end Rhy. Fig. 1

Keybd. 2 *(arr. for gtr.)*

Rhy. Fig. 1A

end Rhy. Fig. 1A

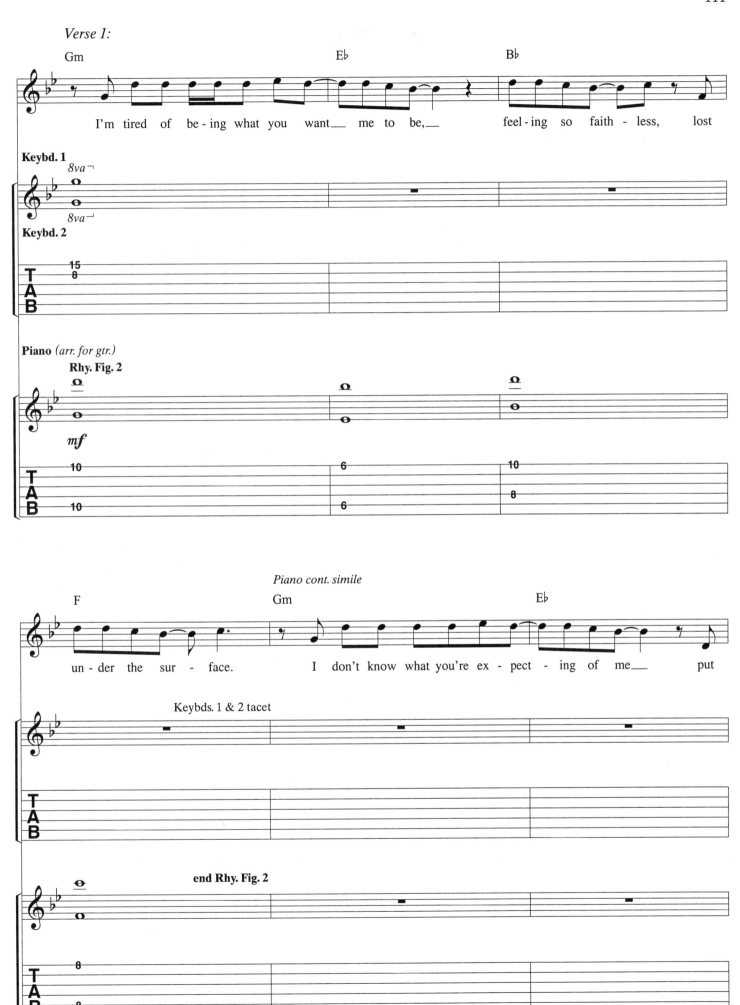

Numb - 8 - 2

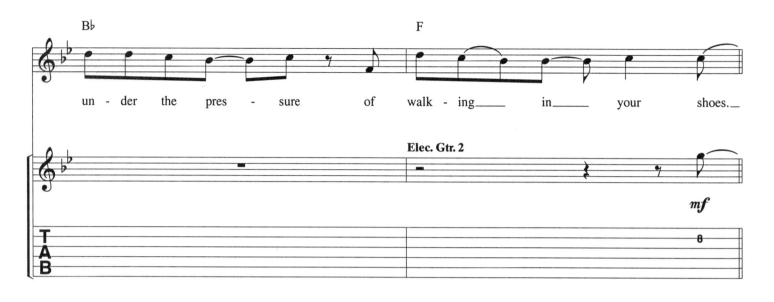

un - der   the   pres - sure   of   walk - ing____   in____   your   shoes.__

Pre-chorus 1:

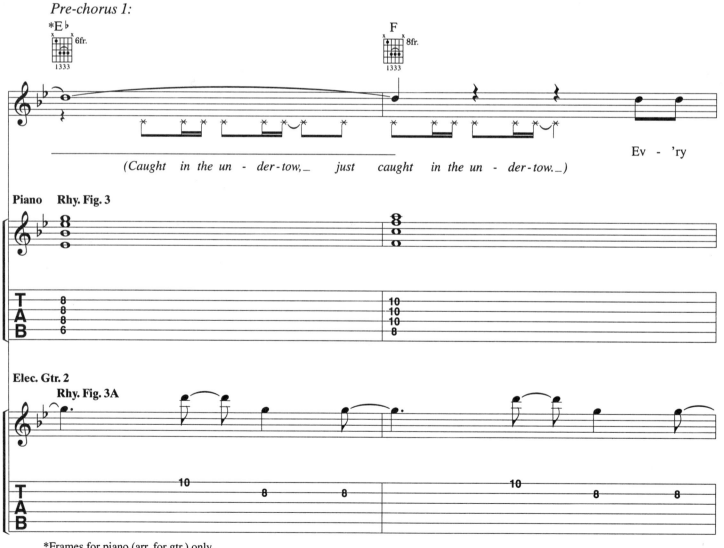

(*Caught   in the un - der - tow,_   just   caught   in the un - der - tow._*)

Ev - 'ry

*Frames for piano (arr. for gtr.) only.

Pre-chorus 2:
w/Rhy. Figs. 3 *(Piano)* **& 3A** *(Elec. Gtr. 2) both 2 times*

Eb   F
(Caught in the un-der-tow,__ just caught in the un-der-tow.__)   Ev-'ry

Gm   Bb
step that I take____ is an-oth-er mis-take____ to you.__

Eb   F
(Caught in the un-der-tow,__ just caught in the un-der-tow.__)   And ev-'ry

Chorus:
w/Rhy. Figs. 1 *(Elec. Gtr. 1)* **& 1A** *(Keybd. 2)*

Gm   Bb   G5
sec-ond I waste__ is more than I can take.____ I've be-come so____

Eb5   Bb5/F   F5   G5
numb, I can't feel you there, be-come so____ tired, so much more a-ware. I'm be-com-ing

Bridge:
w/Rhy. Fig. 1A *(Keybd. 2)*
1 1/2 times

Eb5   Bb5/F   F5   Eb5
Elec.
Gtr. 1 ◇
this, all I want to do is be more like me and be less like you.   And I know__

Numb - 8 - 6

116

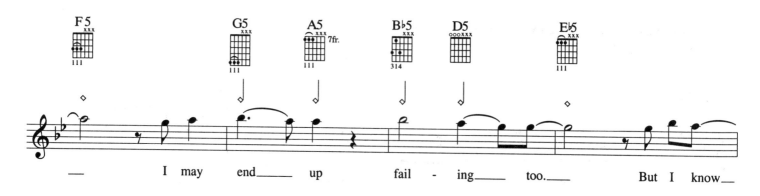

I may end___ up fail - ing___ too.___ But I know___

you were just like_ me___ with some - one dis - ap - point - ed in you.___

Keybd. 2

D.S. 𝄋 al Coda

Coda

me and be less like

Keybd. 1

Numb - 8 - 7

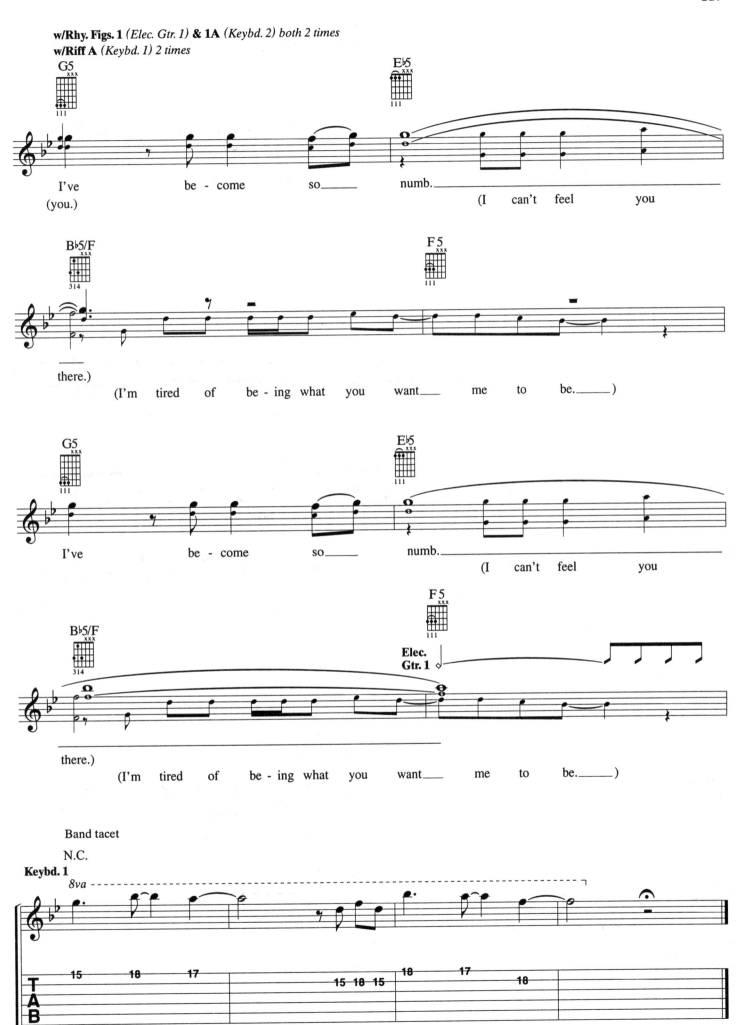

PRAYER

Words and Music by
DAVID DRAIMAN, DAN DONEGAN,
FUZZ and MIKE WENGREN

All gtrs. tune down 1/2 step w/Drop D tuning:

⑥ = D♭   ③ = G♭
⑤ = A♭   ② = B♭
④ = D♭   ① = E♭

♩ = 98   *Intro:*

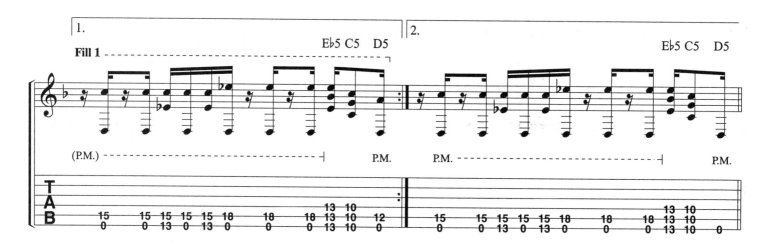

Verse :

1. An-oth-er dream_ that will nev - er come true, just to com - ple - ment_ your sor - row.
2. An-oth-er night - mare a - bout to come true will man - i - fest to-mor - row.

P.M.

*Bass gtr. only

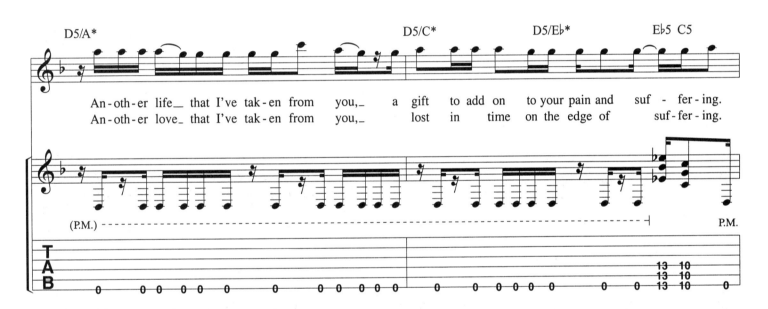

An-oth-er life_ that I've tak-en from you,_ a gift to add on to your pain and suf - fer - ing.
An-oth-er love_ that I've tak-en from you,_ lost in time on the edge of suf - fer - ing.

(P.M.)

An-oth-er, truth that you can nev-er be - lieve has crip - pled you_ com - plete - ly.
An-oth-er taste of the e - vil I breed will la - bel you_ com - plete - ly.

P.M.

120

All the cries you're be-gin-ning to hear,_ trapped in your mind_ and the sound is deaf-en-ing.
Bring to life ev-'ry-thing that you fear._ Live in the dark_ and the world is threat-en-ing. }

Pre-chorus:

Let me_ en-light-en_ you._

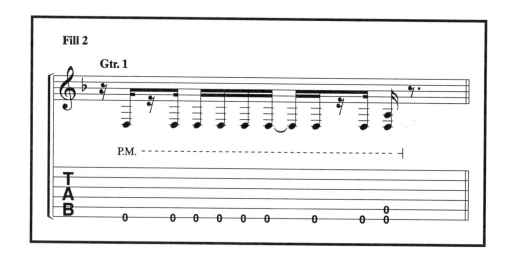

122

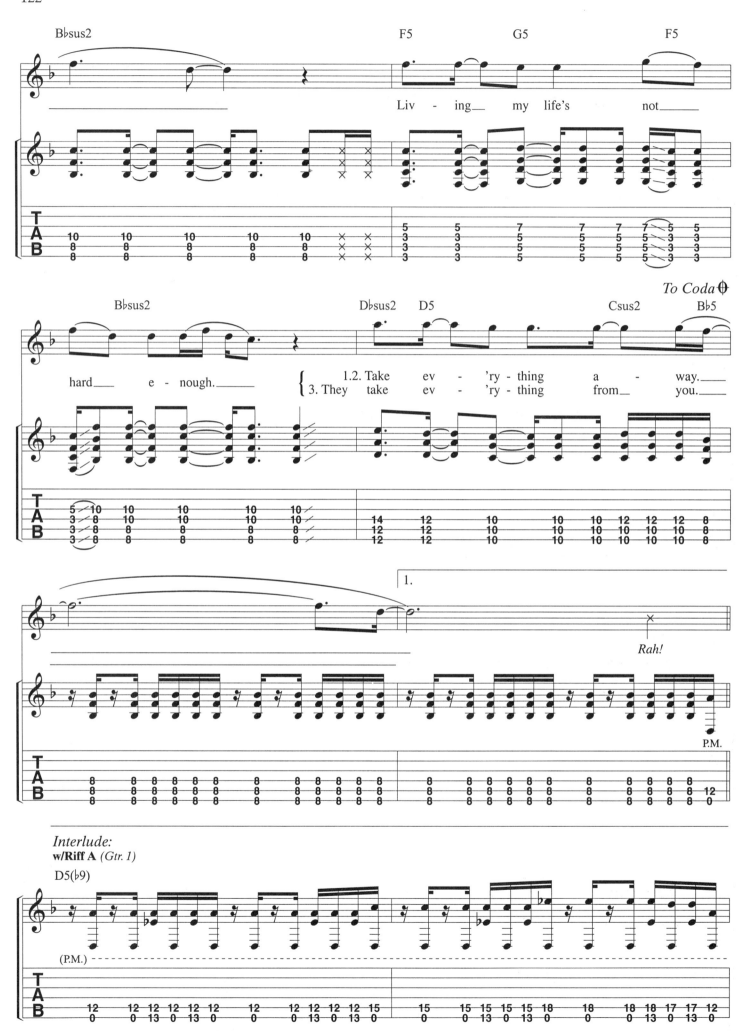

124

PRICE TO PLAY

Music by MICHAEL MUSHOK,
AARON LEWIS, JOHN APRIL
and JONATHAN WYSOCKI
Lyrics by AARON LEWIS

All gtrs. tuned to:
⑥ = Gb ③ = Db
⑤ = Db ② = Gb
④ = Ab ① = Bb

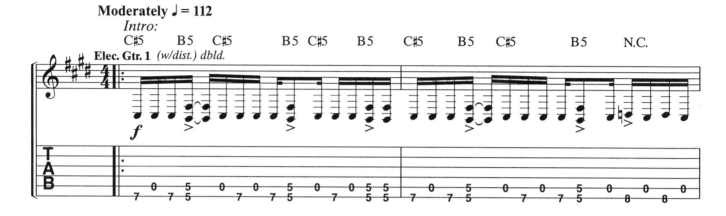

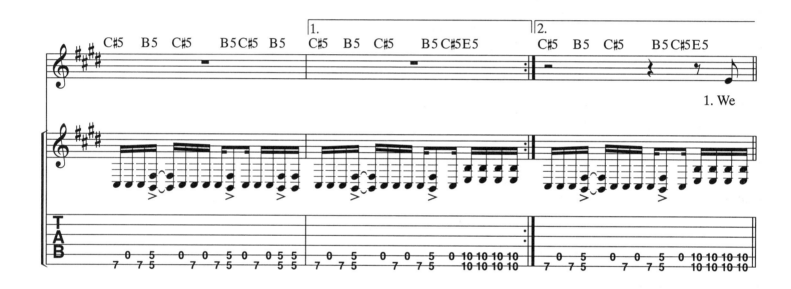

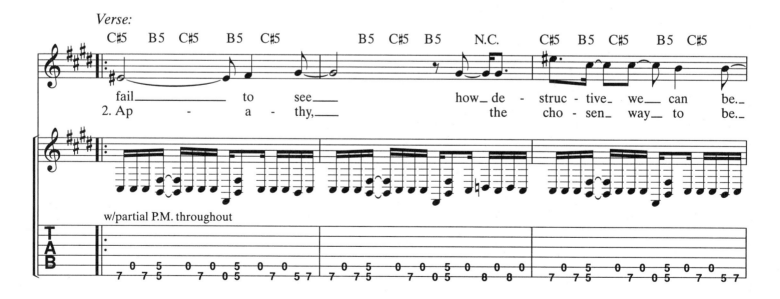

Price to Play - 4 - 1

Price to Play - 4 - 2

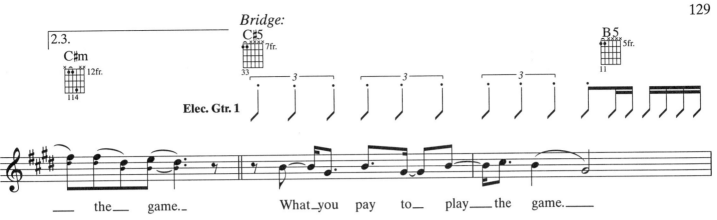

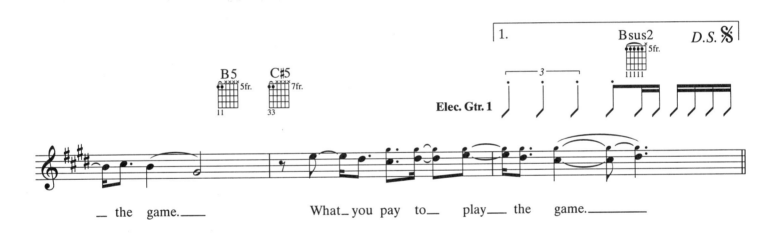

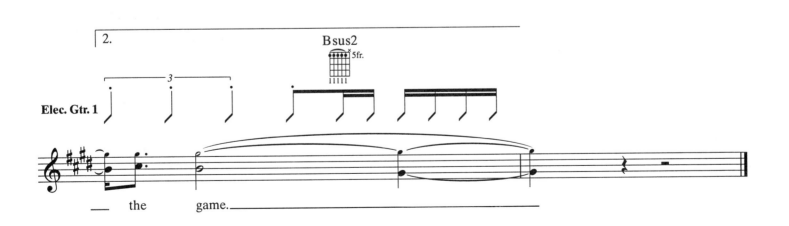

THE RED

Words by PETE LOEFFLER
Music by CHEVELLE

*Tune all gtrs. down 1 1/2 steps:

⑥ = C♯   ③ = E
⑤ = F♯   ② = G♯
④ = B   ① = C♯

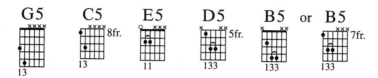

Moderately fast ♩ = 140

Intro:

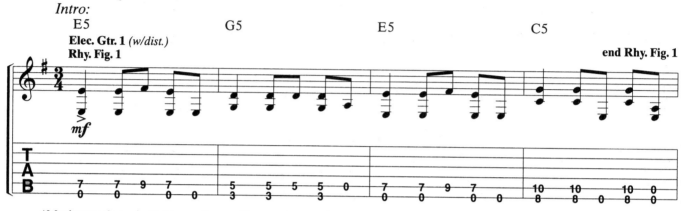

*Music sounds a min. 3rd lower than written.

Verse 1:

w/Rhy. Fig. 1 *(Elec. Gtr. 2 w/dist.) 3 1/2 times, simile*

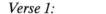

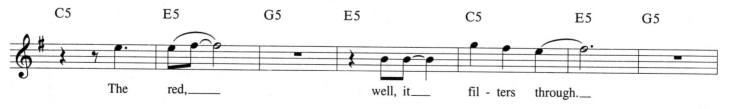

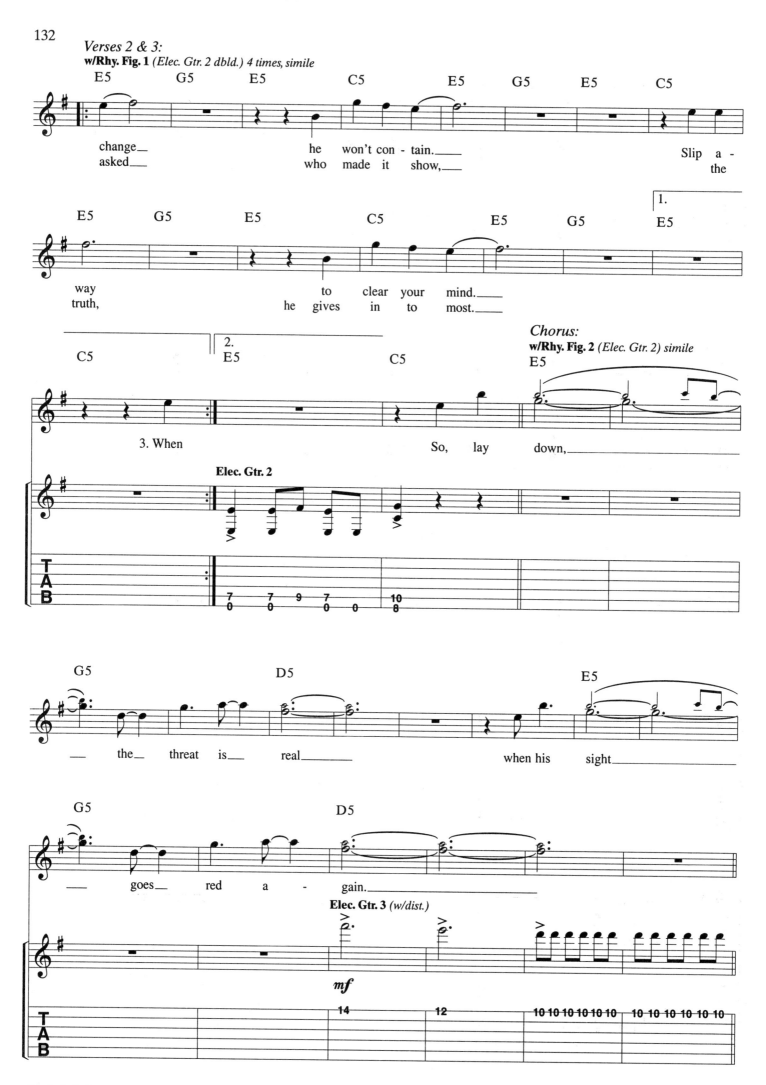

*Two gtrs. arranged for one gtr.

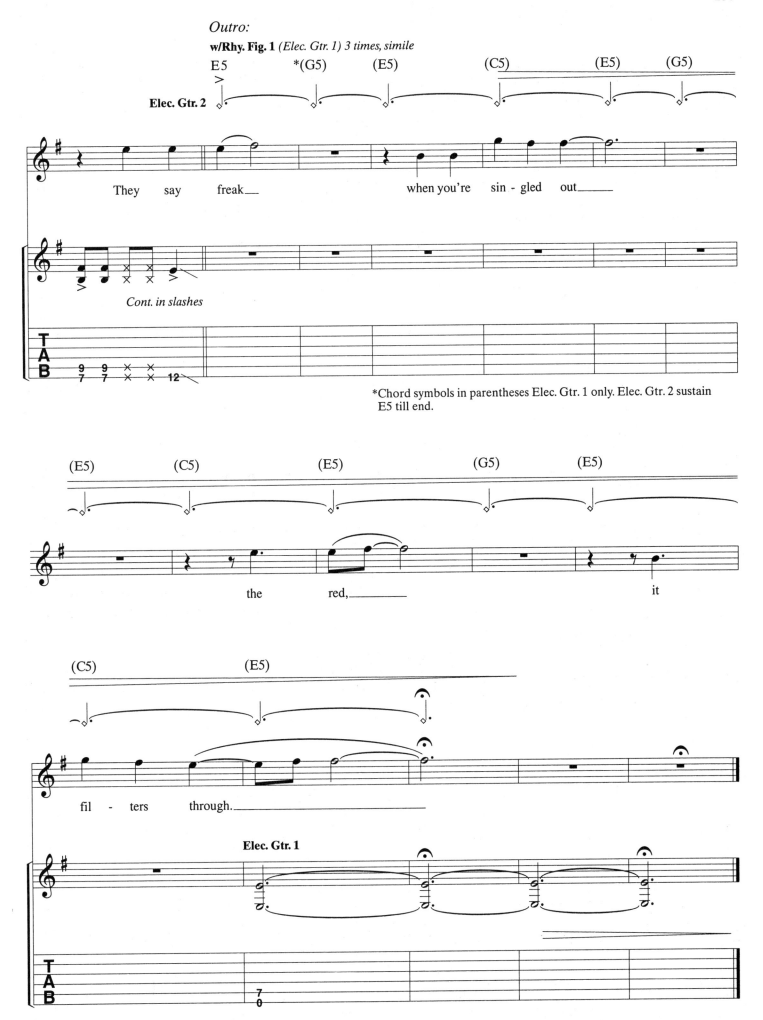

*Chord symbols in parentheses Elec. Gtr. 1 only. Elec. Gtr. 2 sustain E5 till end.

REMEMBER

Words and Music by
DAVID DRAIMAN,
DAN DONEGAN,
FUZZ and
MIKE WENGREN

1. Sen - sa - tion wash - es o - ver_ me,_
2. Blind your eyes to what_ you_ see,_

138

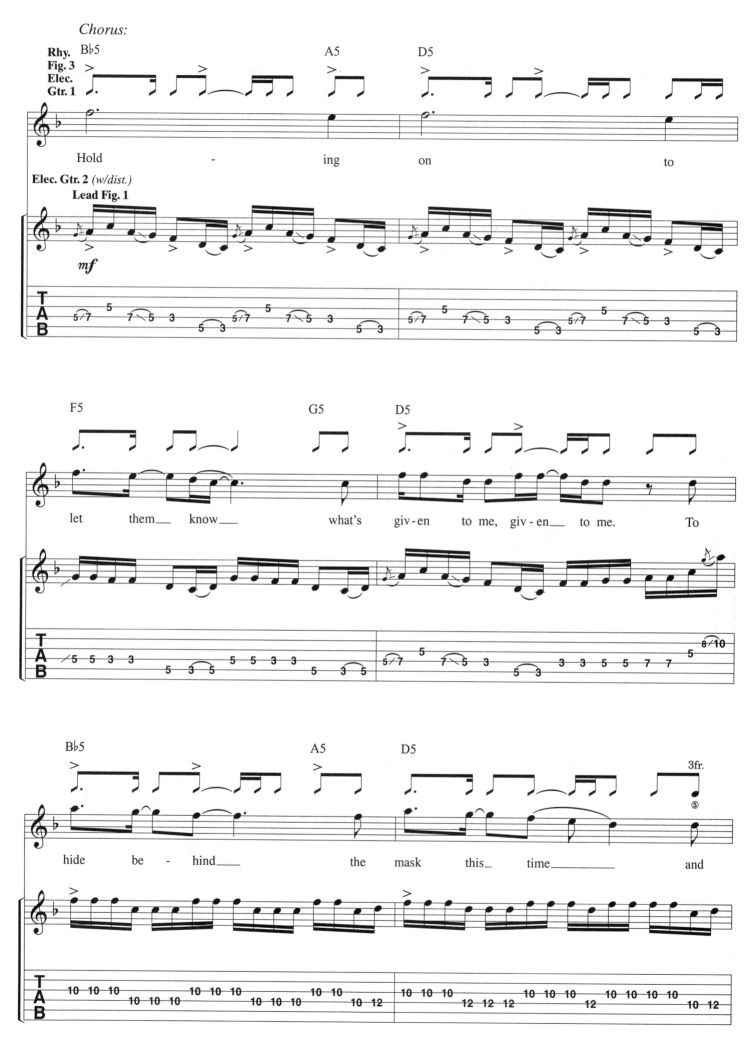

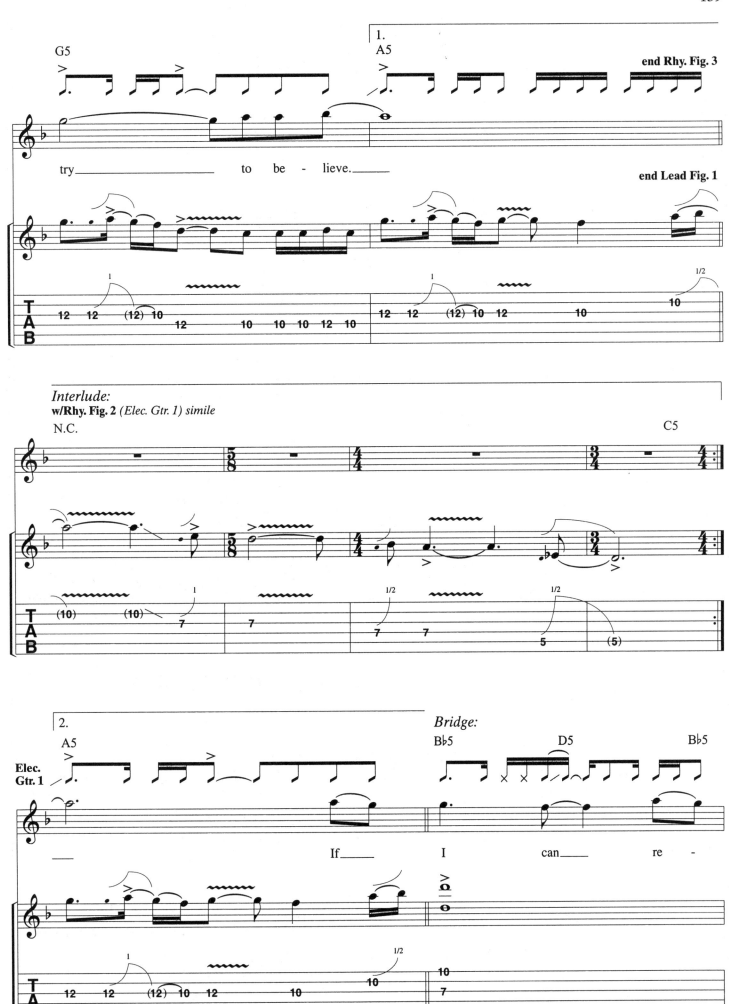

140

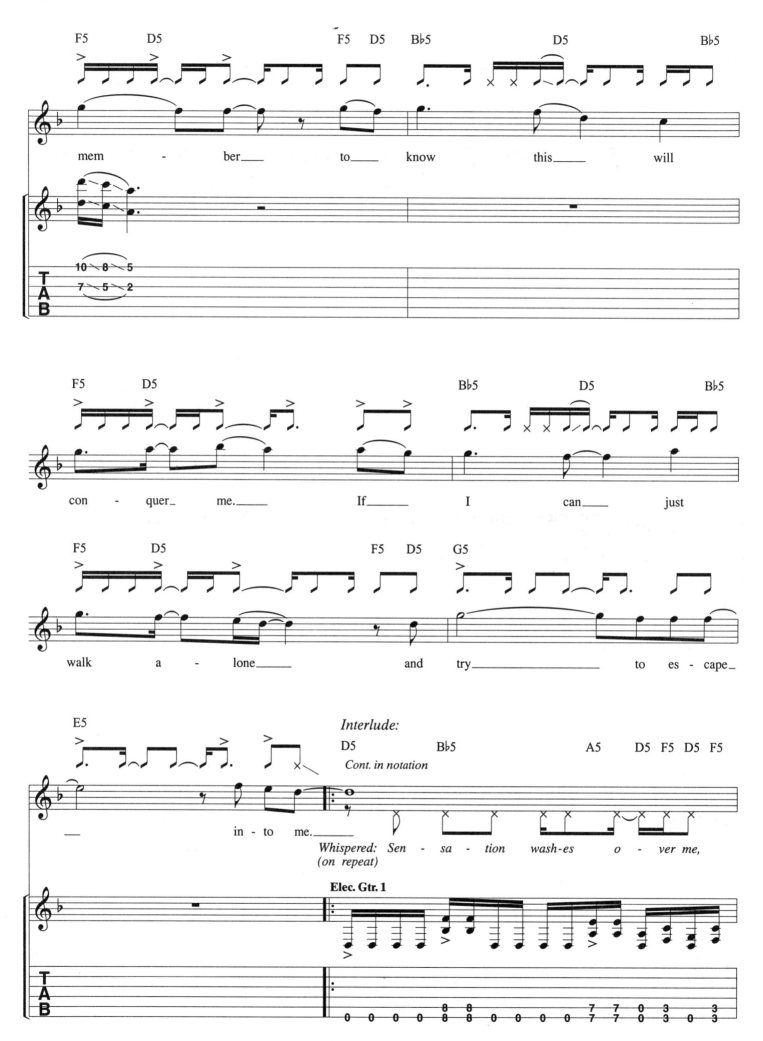

mem - ber___ to___ know this___ will

con - quer___ me.___ If___ I can___ just

walk a - lone___ and try___ to es - cape___

___ in - to me.___

Interlude:
Cont. in notation

Whispered: Sen - sa - tion wash-es o - ver me,
(on repeat)

Elec. Gtr. 1

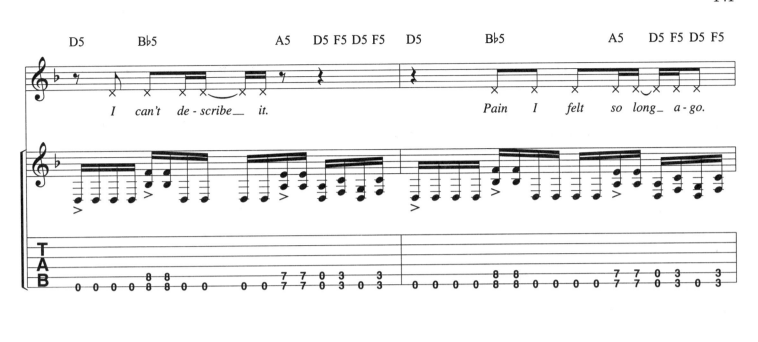

Chorus:
w/Rhy. Fig. 3 (Elec. Gtr. 1) simile
*w/Lead Fig. 1 (Elec. Gtr. 2) simile

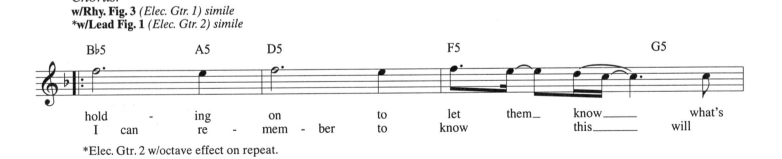

*Elec. Gtr. 2 w/octave effect on repeat.

Remember - 7 - 6

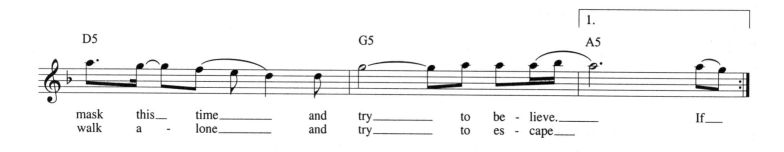

mask this__ time_____ and try_____ to be - lieve._____ If__
walk a - lone_____ and try_____ to es - cape___

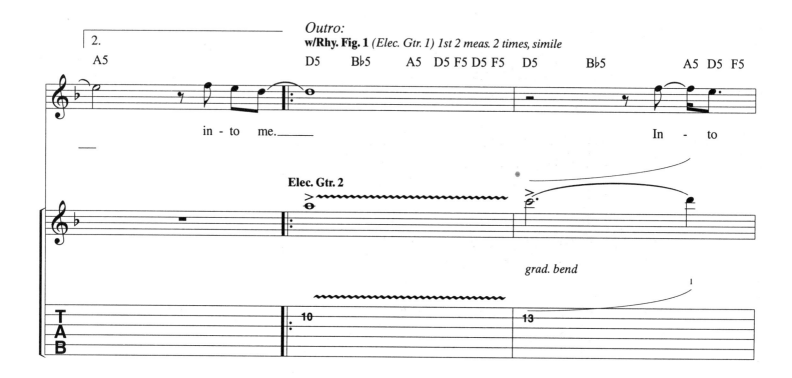

Outro:
w/Rhy. Fig. 1 (Elec. Gtr. 1) 1st 2 meas. 2 times, simile

in - to me._____ In - to

Elec. Gtr. 2

grad. bend

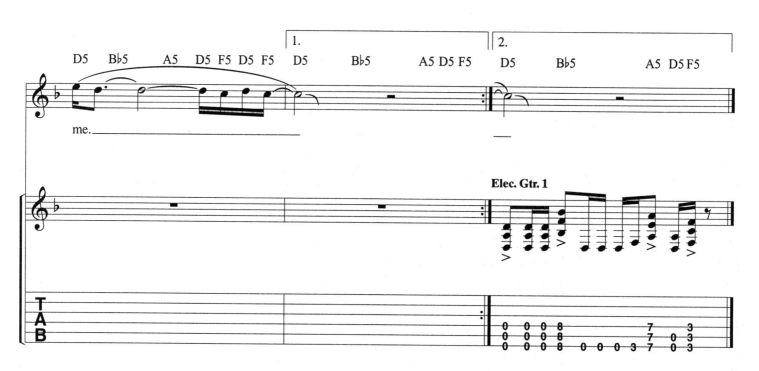

me._____

Elec. Gtr. 1

Someday

Someday - 5 - 3

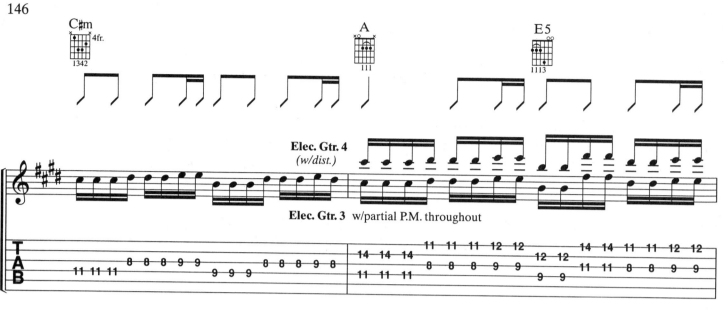

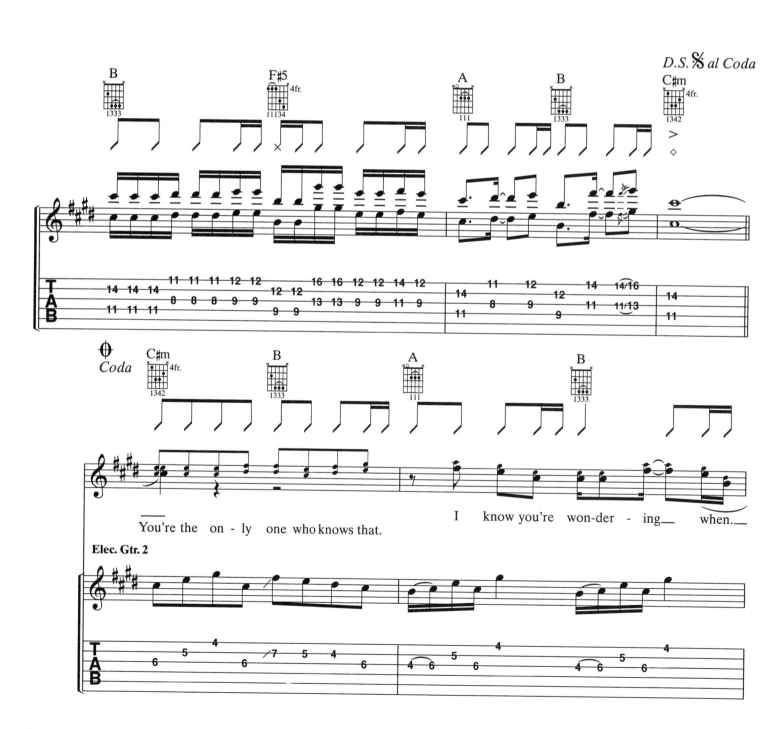

You're the on - ly one who knows that.

I know you're won-der - ing___ when.___

Elec. Gtr. 2

You're the on - ly one who knows that.

I know you're won-der - ing__ when.__

(cont. hold till end)

F#5

Verse 3:
How the hell did we wind up like this?
And why weren't we able to see the signs that we missed
And try to turn the tables?
Now the story's played out like this,
Just like a paperback novel.
Let's rewrite an ending that fits,
Instead of a Hollywood horror.
Nothing's wrong just as long as you know
That someday I will.
(To Chorus:)

THE ROAD I'M ON

Words and Music by
BRAD ARNOLD, ROBERT TODD HARRELL,
CHRISTOPHER LEE HENDERSON
and MATTHEW DARRICK ROBERTS

The Road I'm On - 8 - 2

150

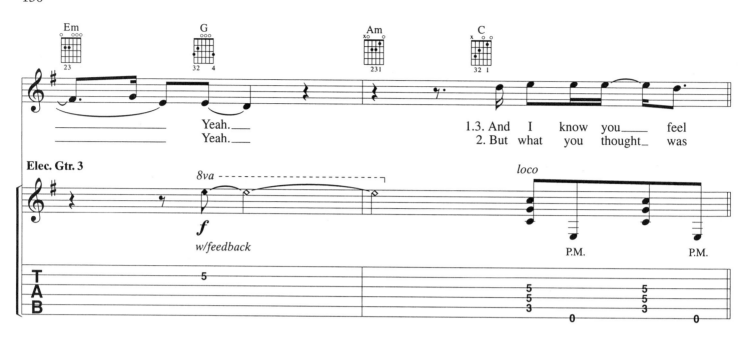

The Road I'm On - 8 - 3

151

The Road I'm On - 8 - 4

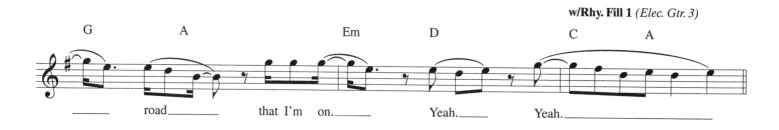

w/Rhy. Fill 1 *(Elec. Gtr. 3)*

G   A   Em   D   C   A

_____ road_____ that I'm on._____ Yeah._____ Yeah._____

Guitar Solo:

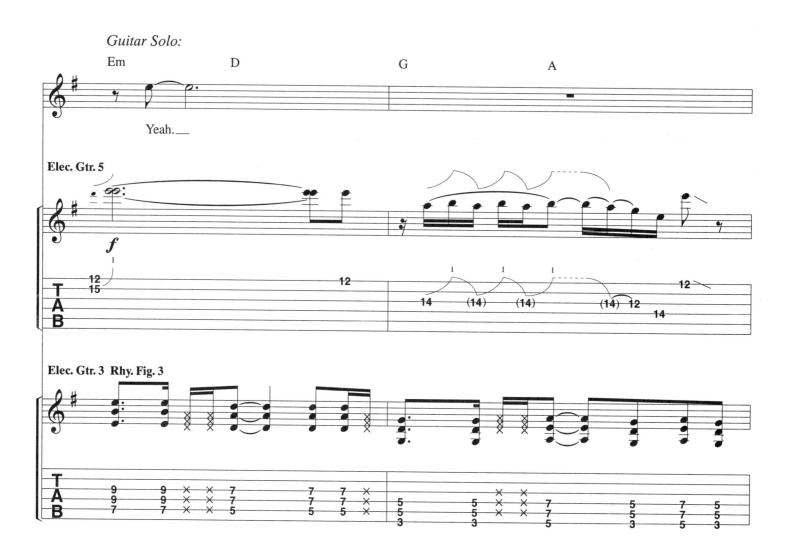

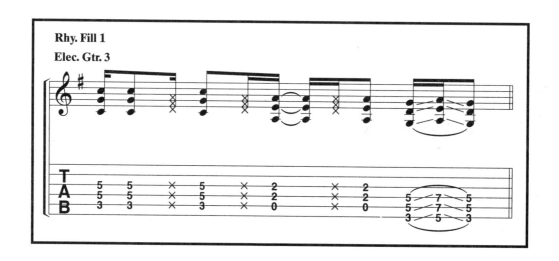

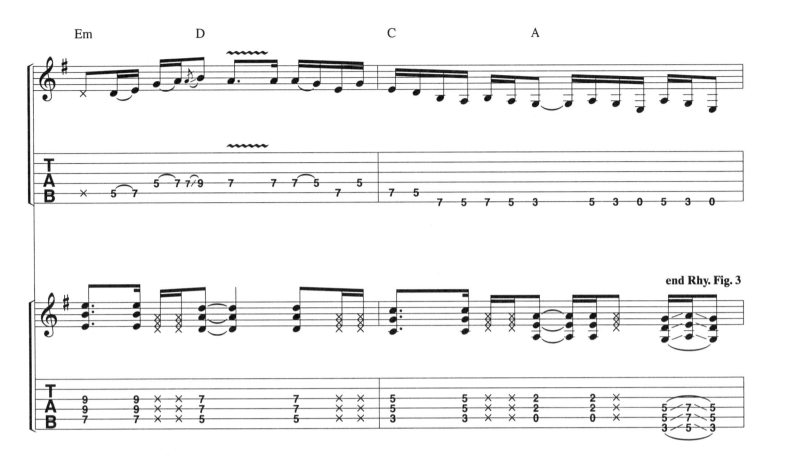

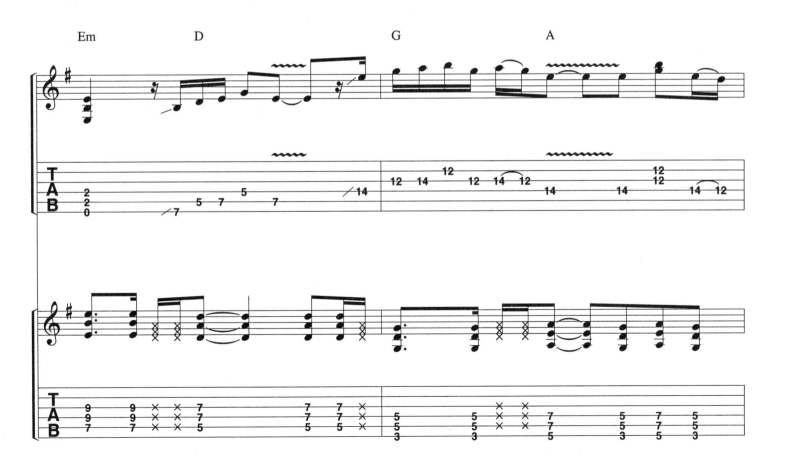

154

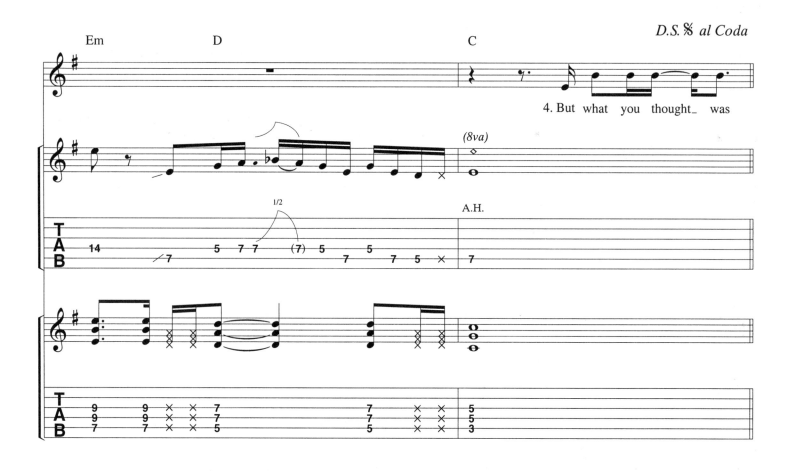

4. But what you thought_ was

Outro:
w/Rhy. Fig. 3 (Elec. Gtr. 3) 2 times

Coda

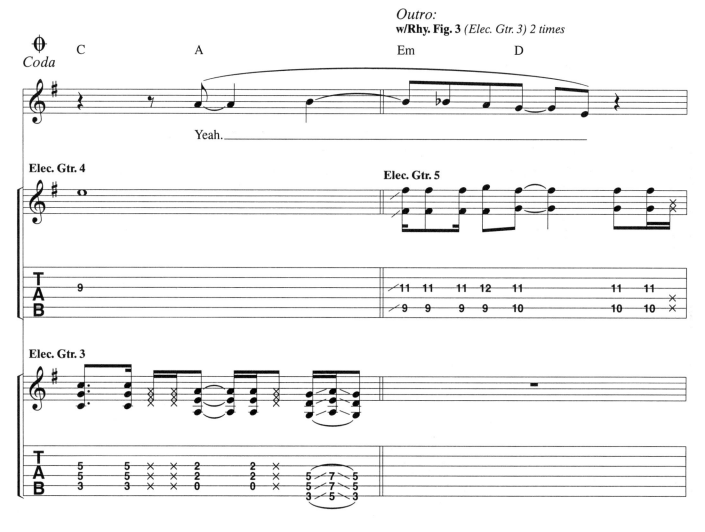

Yeah.

Verse 4:
But what you thought was real in life,
Somehow steered you wrong.
And now you just keep driving, trying to find,
Where you belong.
(To Chorus:)

SEND THE PAIN BELOW

*All gtrs. in Drop D, down 1 1/2 steps:

⑥ = B   ③ = E
⑤ = F#   ② = G#
④ = B   ① = C#

Words by PETE LOEFFLER
Music by CHEVELLE

Moderately ♩ = 92

*Music sounds a min. 3rd lower than written.

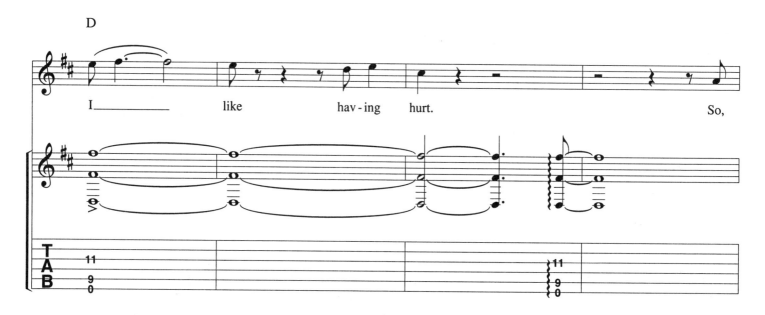

I_____   like   hav-ing   hurt.   So,

Send the Pain Below - 4 - 1

SERENITY

All gtrs. in Drop D tuning:
⑥ = D   ③ = G
⑤ = A   ② = B
④ = D   ① = E

Words and Music by
SULLY ERNA and TONY ROMBOLA

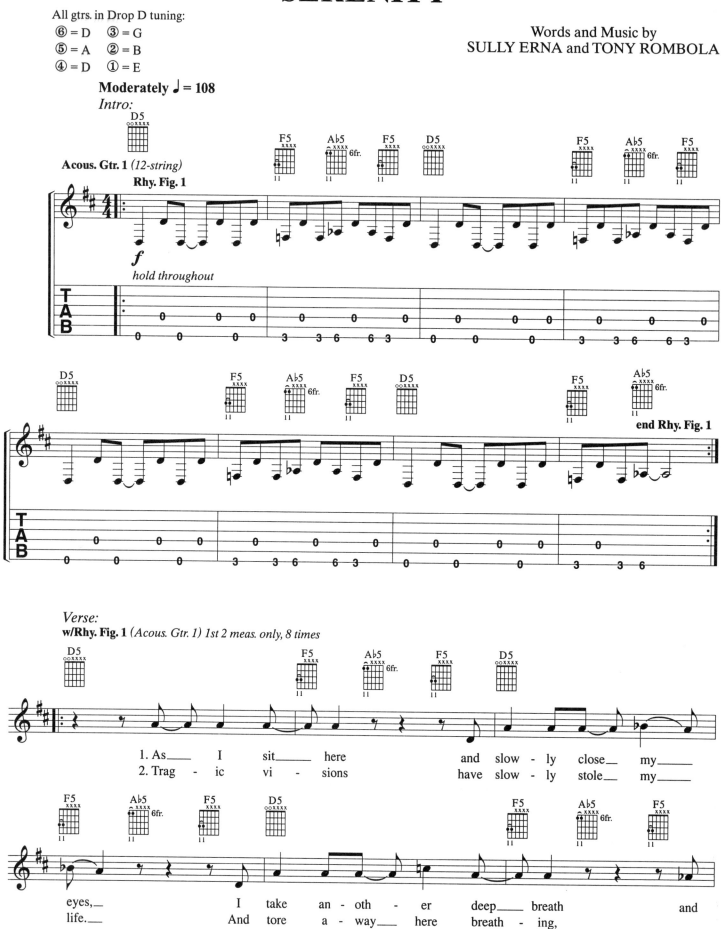

162

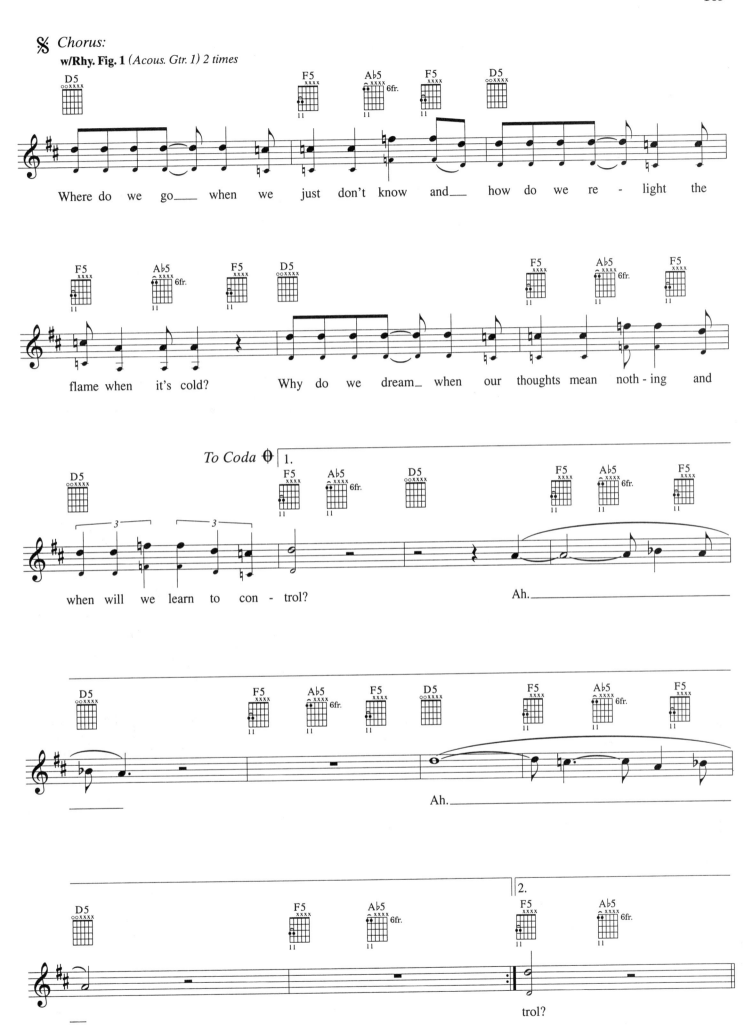

164

SHE HATES ME

All gtrs. tune down 1/2 step:

⑥ = E♭   ③ = G♭
⑤ = A♭   ② = B♭
④ = D♭   ① = E♭

Words and Music by
WESLEY SCANTLIN and JIMMY ALLEN

She Hates Me - 4 - 1

Verse 3:

w/Rhy. Fig. 1 *(Elec. Gtr. 1) 4 times*

That's my sto - ry as you see,__ learned my les - son and

w/Rhy. Fig. 2 *(Elec. Gtr. 2) 1st 4 meas. only*

so did she.__ Now it's o - ver and I'm glad__

D.S. 𝄋 *al Coda*

Coda

Bkgd. Vocal Fig. 1 - - - - - - - - - - -

'cause I'm a fool for all I've said.__ She f***-in'

(La - la - la - la - la - la -

w/Bkgd. Vocal Fig. 1, *3 times*

(Rhy. Fig. 1) - - - - - - - - - - - - - - - -

la - la - la - la.__) Trust, as she

Elec.
Gtr. 3

tore my feel-ings like I had none. She f***-in' hates me!

SO FAR AWAY

Elec. Gtrs. 1 & 2 tuned:

⑥ = A♭   ③ = D♭
⑤ = E♭   ② = E♭
④ = A♭   ① = A♭

Acous. Gtr. 1 & Elec. Gtr. 3 tuned down 1/2 step:

⑥ = E♭   ③ = G♭
⑤ = A♭   ② = B♭
④ = D♭   ① = E♭

Music by MICHAEL MUSHOK,
AARON LEWIS, JOHN APRIL
and JONATHAN WYSOCKI
Lyrics by AARON LEWIS

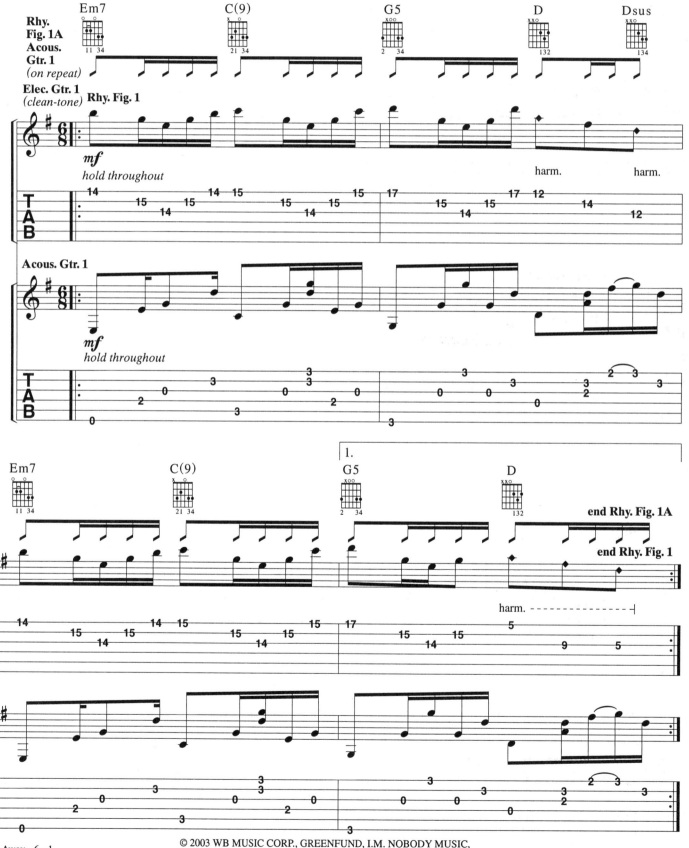

172

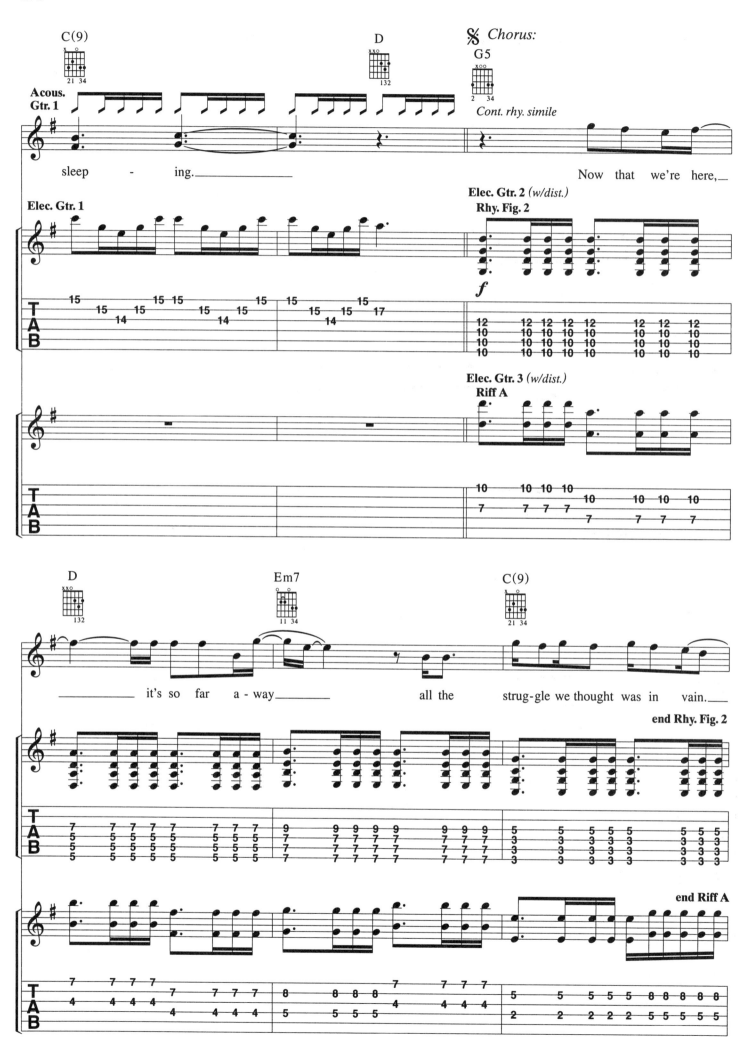

174

So Far Away - 6 - 5

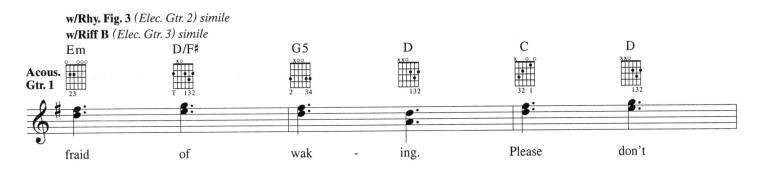

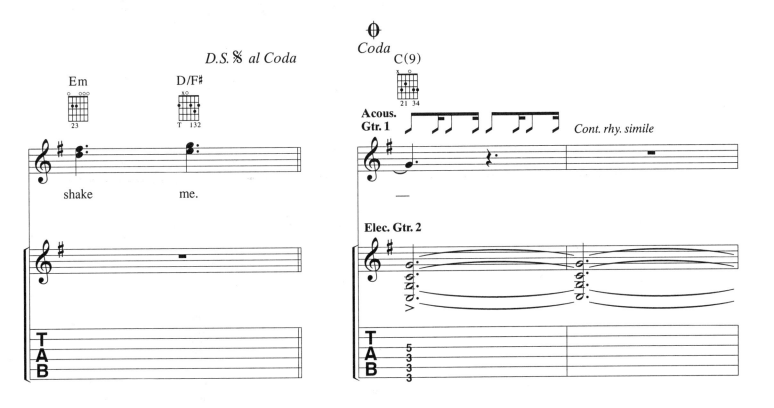

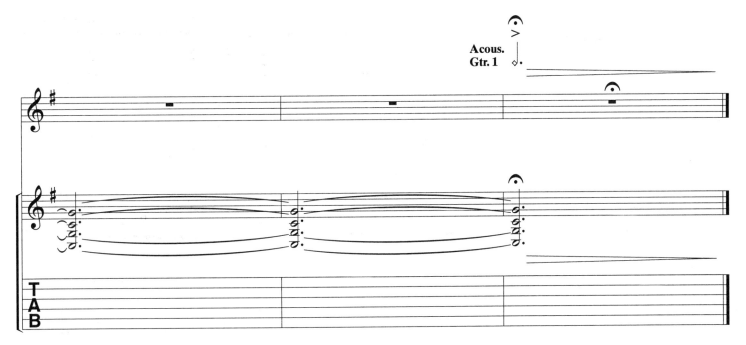

SOMEWHERE I BELONG

By LINKIN PARK

Tune down 1/2 step:

⑥ = E♭   ③ = G♭

⑤ = A♭   ② = B♭

④ = D♭   ① = E♭

Moderate rock ♩ = 80

Intro:

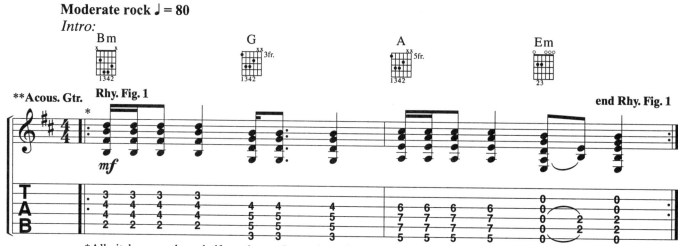

*All pitches sound one half step lower than written (key of B♭ minor).

**Acous. Gtr. part is digitally processed using Pro Tools, creating a "backwards" effect.

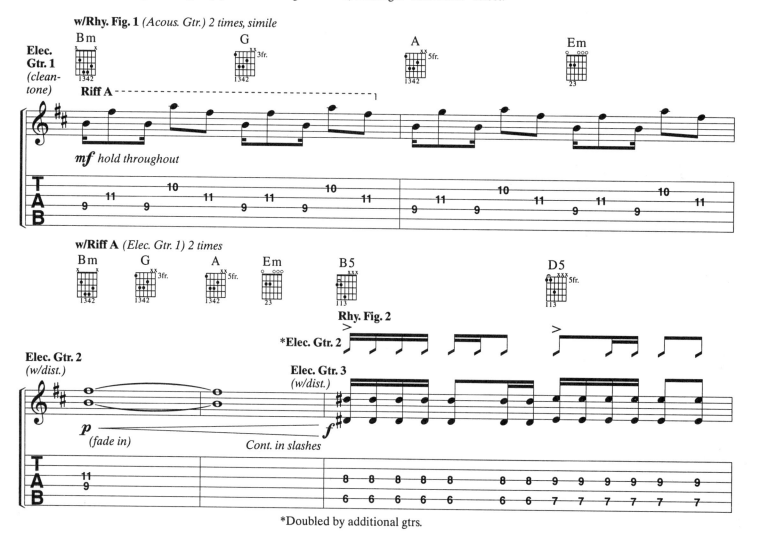

*Doubled by additional gtrs.

180

Somewhere I Belong - 8 - 5

182

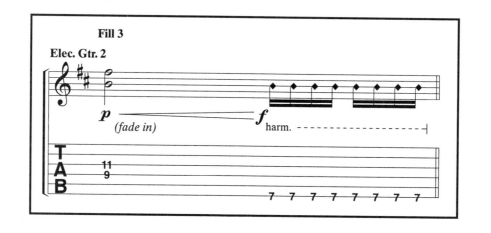

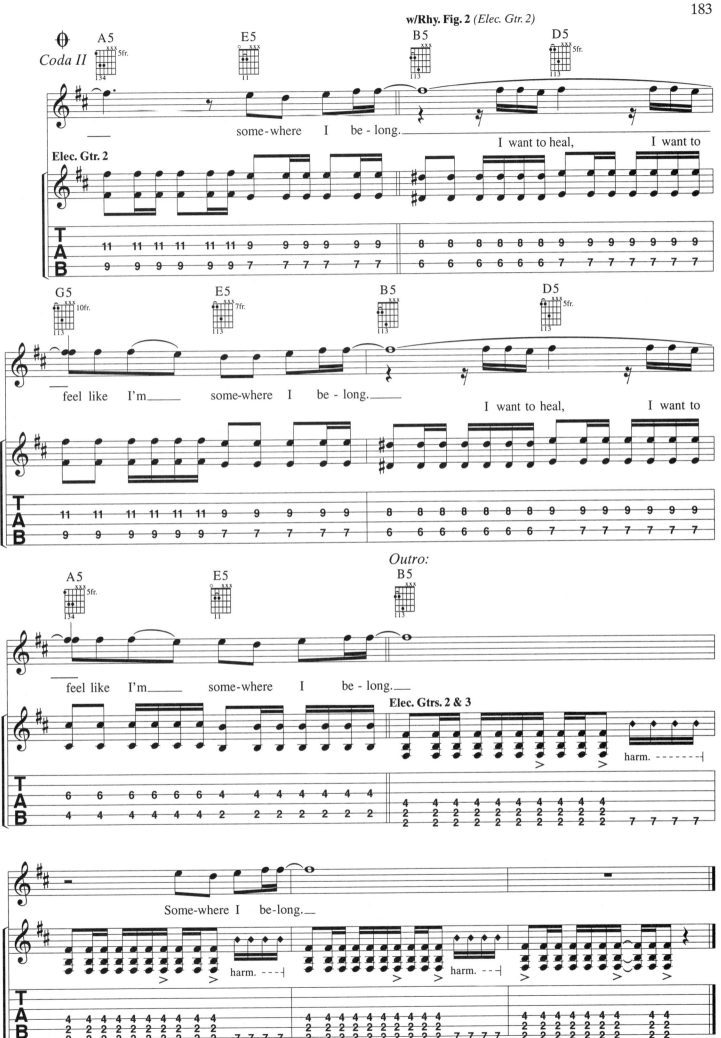

STILL FRAME

All gtrs. are 7-string gtrs. tuned:

⑦ = B ③ = G
⑥ = E ② = B
⑤ = A ① = E
④ = D

Music by
CHRIS BROWN, PETER CHARELL
and SIMON ORMANDY
Lyrics by
CHRIS BROWN

Moderately fast ♩ = 114
Intro:

N.C.

Elec. Gtr. 1 *(clean-tone)*
8vb

mf
w/chorus effect

(8vb)

Cont. in slashes

𝄋 *Chorus:*

**Rhy.
Fig. 1
Elec.
Gtr. 1**
(w/dist.)
dbld.

B5   A5   B5   G5   B5   A5   B5

f   *end Rhy. Fig. 1*

Please____ help____ me 'cause I'm break-ing____ down, this

w/Rhy. Fig. 1 *(Elec. Gtr. 1) 3 times, simile*

A5   B5   G5   B5   A5   B5

pic-ture's____ fro-zen____ and I can't get____ out.

186

188

STRAIGHT OUT OF LINE

All gtrs. in Drop D, down 1 whole step:

⑥ = C ③ = F
⑤ = G ② = A
④ = C ① = D

Words and Music by
SULLY ERNA

Moderate rock ♩ = 92

Intro:
N.C.

*Vol. swells.

w/fdbk.

Riff A

end **Riff A**

P.M.

Straight Out of Line - 8 - 1

-son   why I____ should   jus - ti - fy____ my____ ways.____

____   Straight   out____ of   line,_____   I don't   need   a rea-

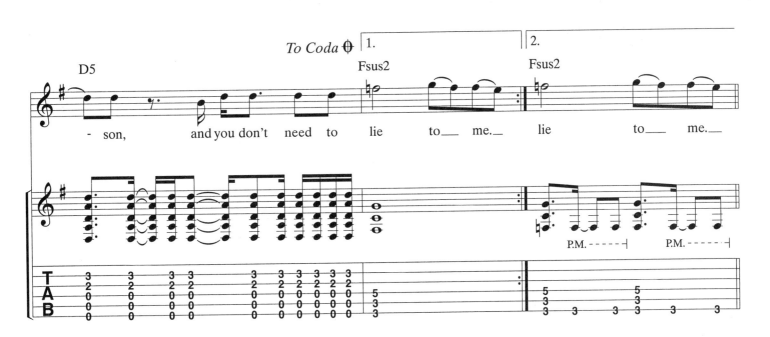

-son,   and you don't   need   to   lie   to____ me.____   lie   to____ me.____

196

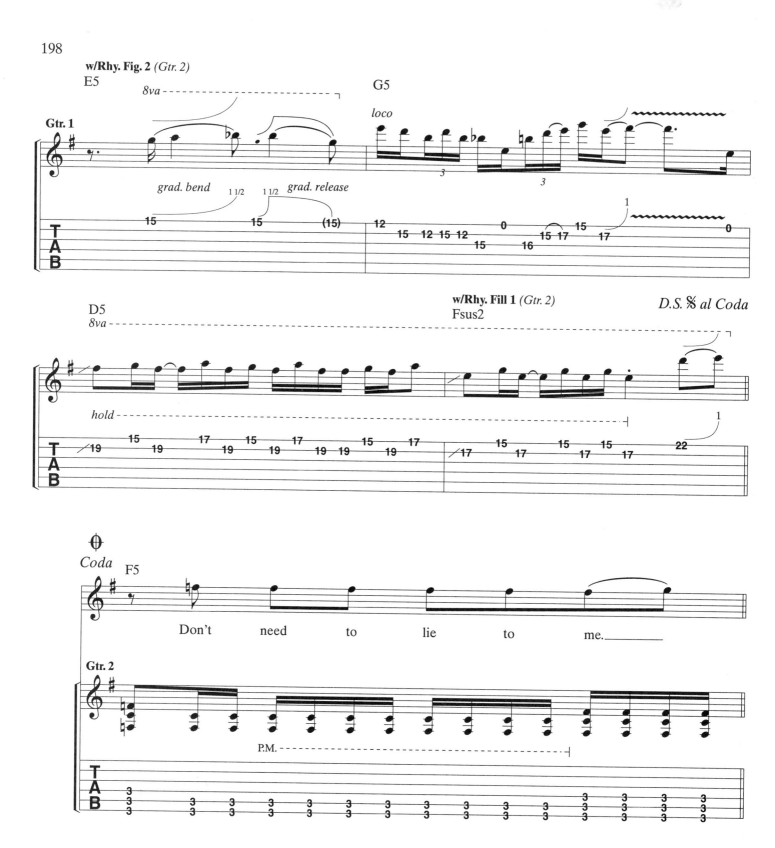

Outro:
w/misc. vocals

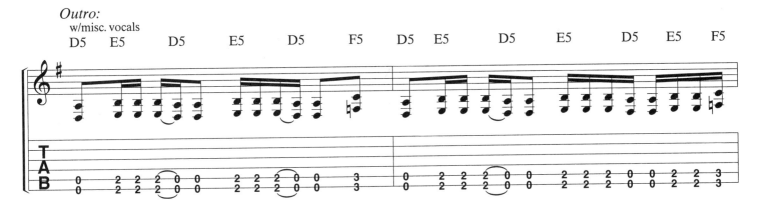

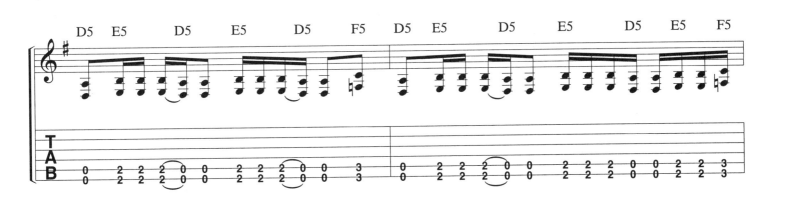

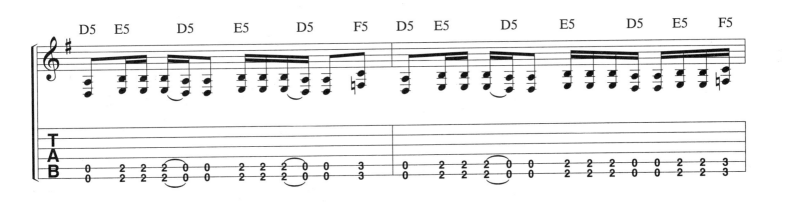

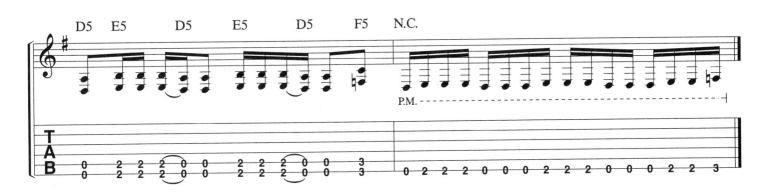

Straight Out of Line - 8 - 8

WHEN I'M GONE

Words and Music by
BRAD ARNOLD, ROBERT TODD HARRELL,
CHRISTOPHER LEE HENDERSON
and MATTHEW DARRICK ROBERTS

Verse 1:

oth - er world__ in - side__ of me__ that you may nev - er see._____ There are

Elec. Gtr. 3
Rhy. Fig. 1

mf
hold throughout

Elec. Gtr. 2
Rhy. Fig. 1A

se - crets in__ this life__ that I__ can't__ hide._____ And

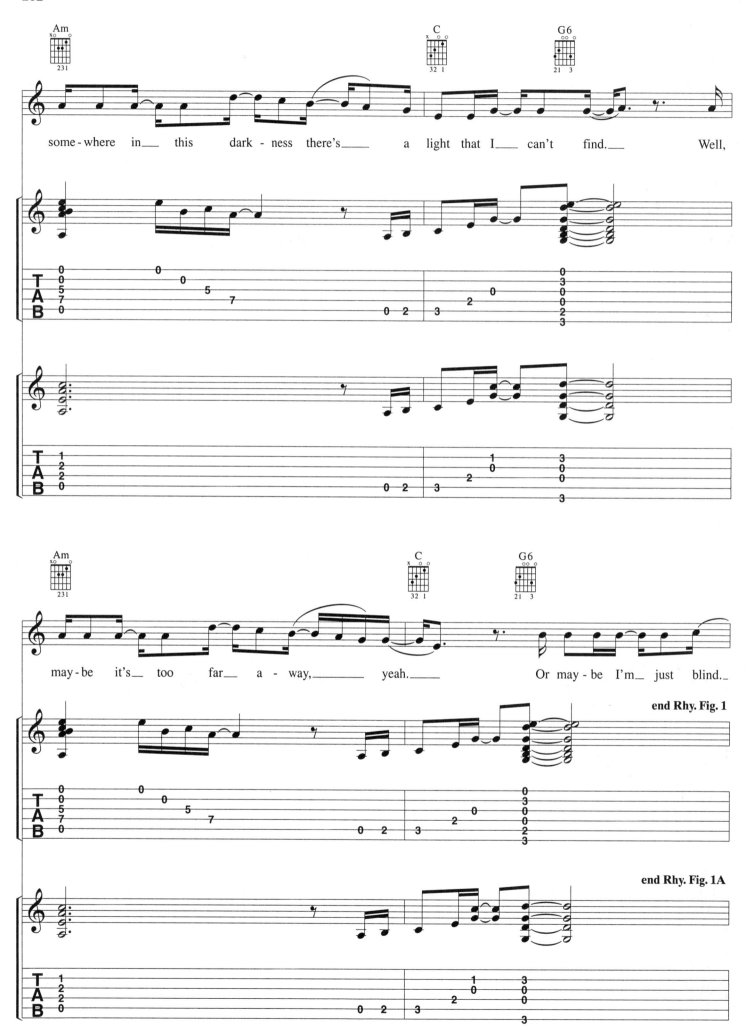

Yeah, may-be I'm__ just blind.__

*Elec. Gtr. 2 & Acous. Gtr.

hold throughout

*Two gtrs. arr. for one.

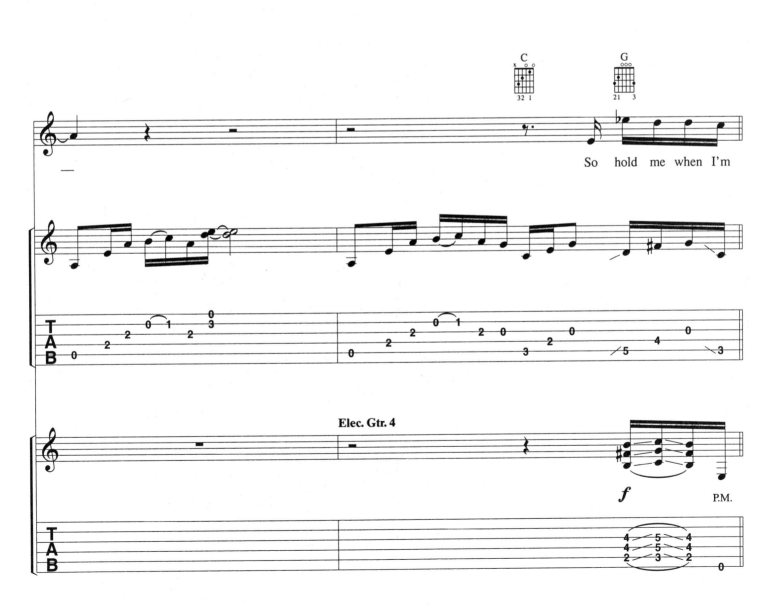

So hold me when I'm

Elec. Gtr. 4

When I'm Gone - 13 - 4

204

% *Chorus:*

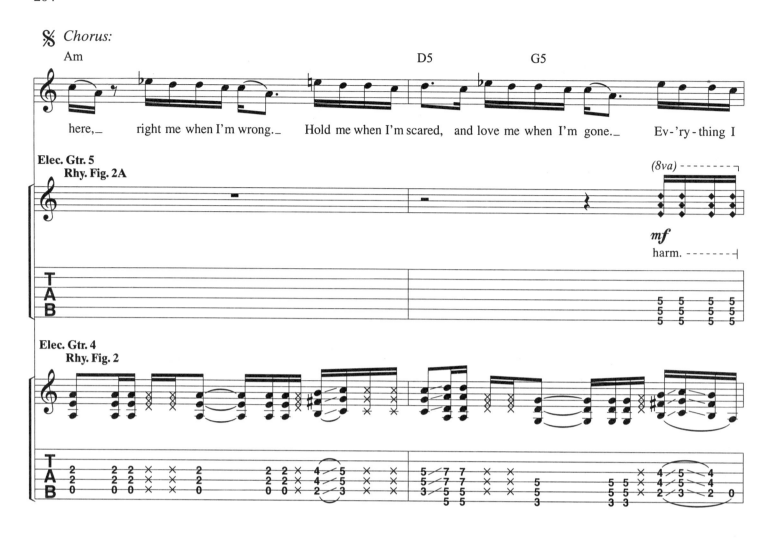

206

When I'm Gone - 13 - 8

208

So hold me when I'm

I'm gone.

209

When I'm Gone - 13 - 10

210

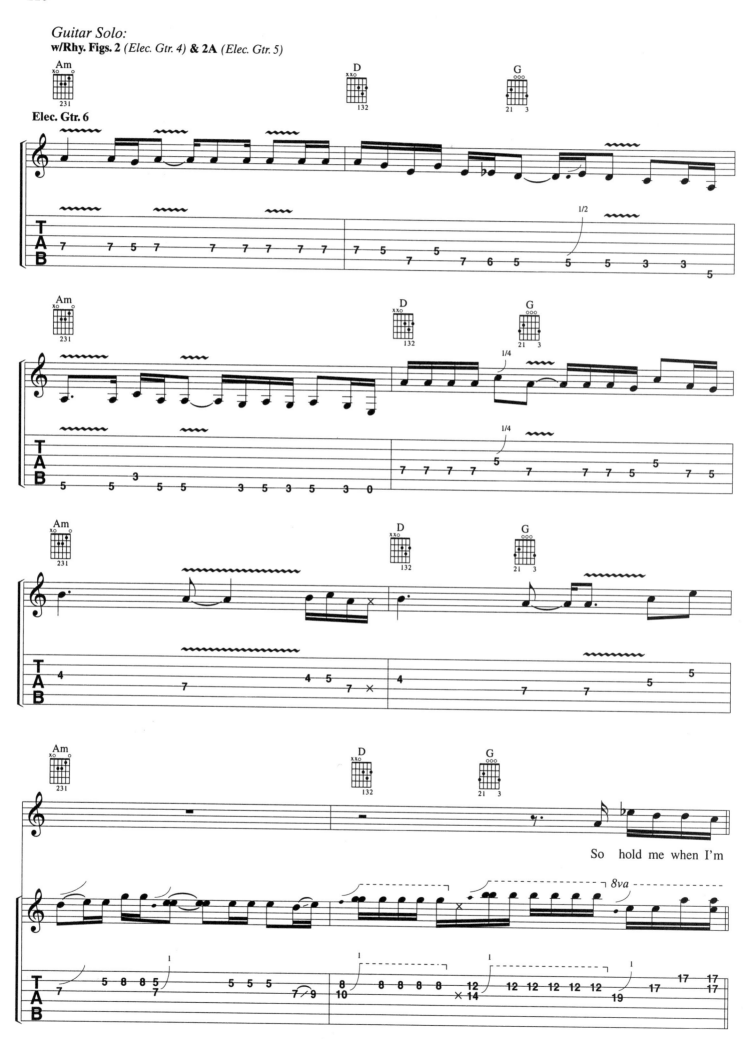

So hold me when I'm

When I'm Gone - 13 - 11

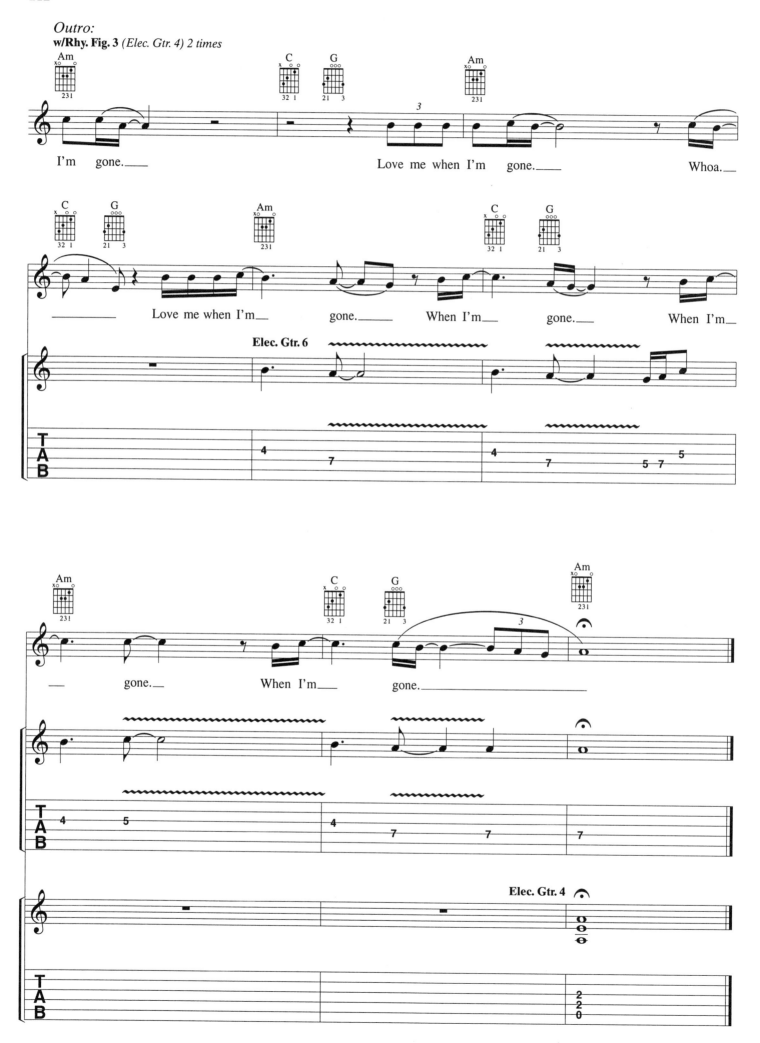

WORLD SO COLD

Words and Music by
MATTHEW McDONOUGH, GREG TRIBBETT,
RYAN MARTINIE and CHAD GRAY

All gtrs. in "Drop D," down 1 whole step:

⑥ = C ③ = F
⑤ = G ② = A
④ = C ① = D

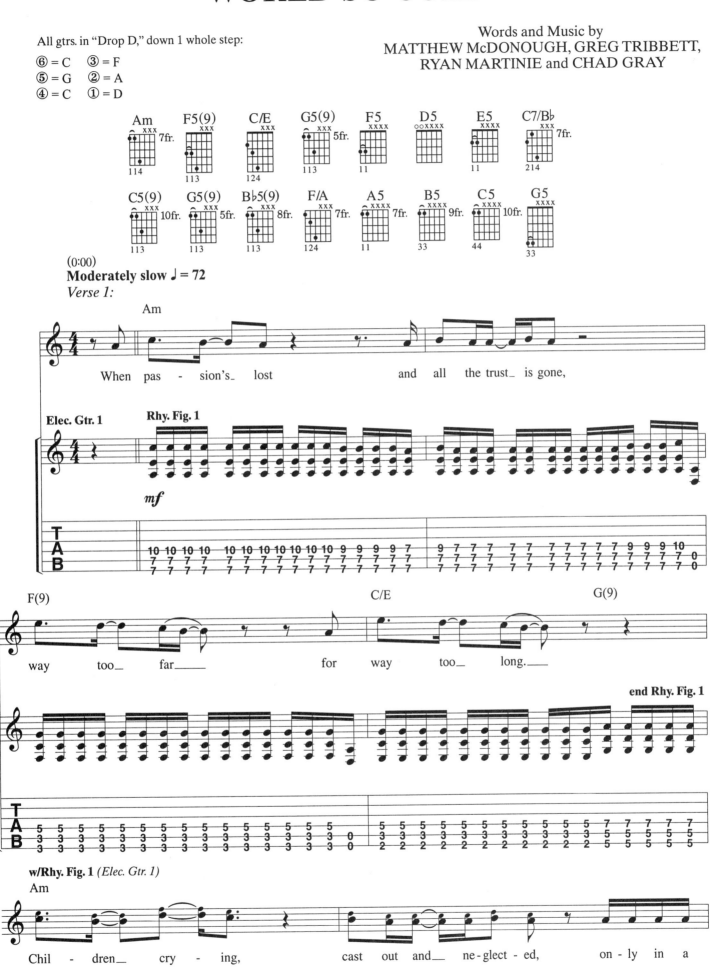

(0:00)
Moderately slow ♩ = 72
Verse 1:

214

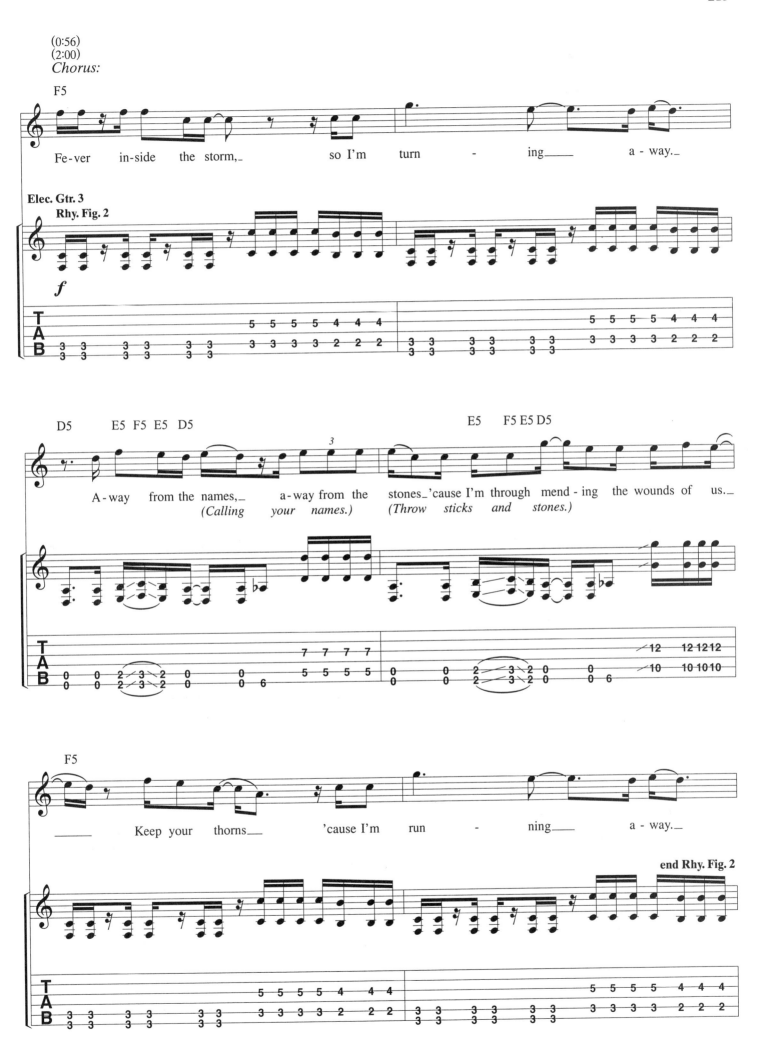

World So Cold - 9 - 3

218

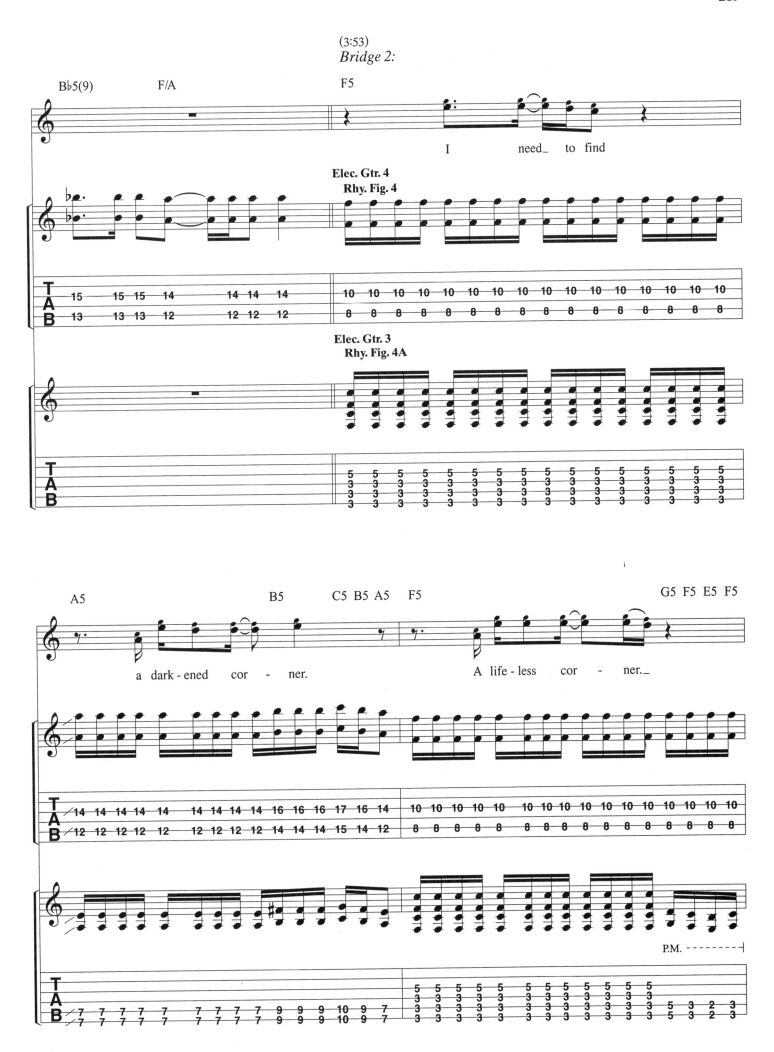

220

WON'T BACK DOWN

All gtrs. tune down 1 whole step w/Drop D tuning:

⑥ = C   ③ = F
⑤ = G   ② = A
④ = C   ① = D

Words and Music by
CARL BELL

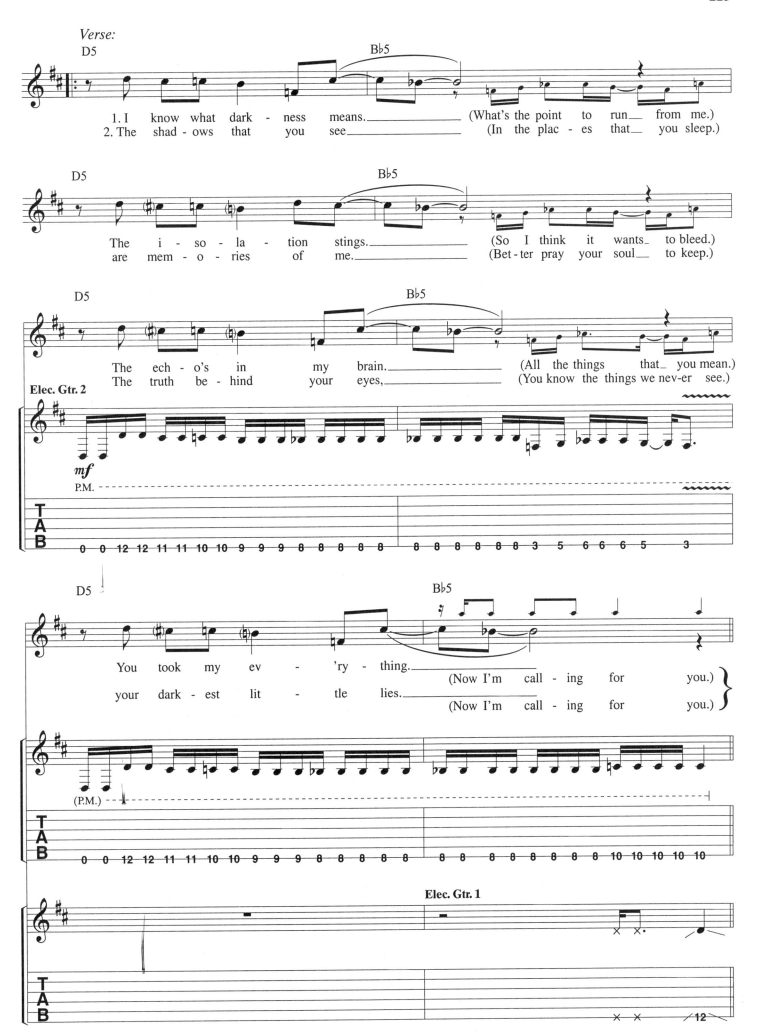

GUITAR TAB GLOSSARY **

TABLATURE EXPLANATION

READING TABLATURE: Tablature illustrates the six strings of the guitar. Notes and chords are indicated by the placement of fret numbers on a given string(s).

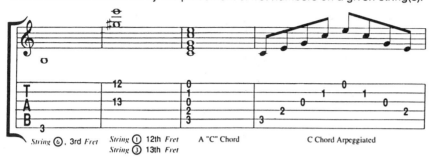

String ⑥, 3rd Fret String ① 12th Fret A "C" Chord   C Chord Arpeggiated
String ③ 13th Fret

BENDING NOTES

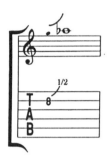

HALF STEP: Play the note and bend string one half step.*

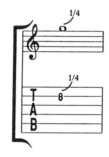

SLIGHT BEND (Microtone): Play the note and bend string slightly to the equivalent of half a fret.

BEND AND RELEASE: Play the note and gradually bend to the next pitch, then release to the original note. Only the first note is attacked.

WHOLE STEP: Play the note and bend string one whole step.

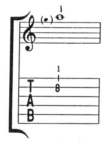

PREBEND (Ghost Bend): Bend to the specified note, before the string is picked.

BENDS INVOLVING MORE THAN ONE STRING: Play the note and bend string while playing an additional note (or notes) on another string(s). Upon release, relieve pressure from additional note(s), causing original note to sound alone.

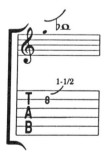

WHOLE STEP AND A HALF: Play the note and bend string a whole step and a half.

PREBEND AND RELEASE: Bend the string, play it, then release to the original note.

BENDS INVOLVING STATIONARY NOTES: Play notes and bend lower pitch, then hold until release begins (indicated at the point where line becomes solid).

UNISON BEND: Play both notes and immediately bend the lower note to the same pitch as the higher note.

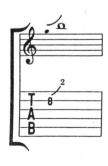

TWO STEPS: Play the note and bend string two whole steps.

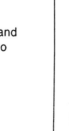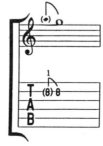

REVERSE BEND: Play the already-bent string, then immediately drop it down to the fretted note.

DOUBLE NOTE BEND: Play both notes and immediately bend both strings simultaneously.

*A half step is the smallest interval in Western music; it is equal to one fret. A whole step equals two frets.

© 1990 Beam Me Up Music
c/o CPP/Belwin, Inc. Miami, Florida 33014
International Copyright Secured   Made in U.S.A.   All Rights Reserved   **By Kenn Chipkin and Aaron Stang

RHYTHM SLASHES

STRUM INDICATIONS: Strum with indicated rhythm.

The chord voicings are found on the first page of the transcription underneath the song title.

INDICATING SINGLE NOTES USING RHYTHM SLASHES: Very often single notes are incorporated into a rhythm part. The note name is indicated above the rhythm slash with a fret number and a string indication.

ARTICULATIONS

HAMMER ON: Play lower note, then "hammer on" to higher note with another finger. Only the first note is attacked.

LEFT HAND HAMMER: Hammer on the first note played on each string with the left hand.

PULL OFF: Play higher note, then "pull off" to lower note with another finger. Only the first note is attacked.

FRET-BOARD TAPPING: "Tap" onto the note indicated by + with a finger of the pick hand, then pull off to the following note held by the fret hand.

TAP SLIDE: Same as fretboard tapping, but the tapped note is slid randomly up the fretboard, then pulled off to the following note.

BEND AND TAP TECHNIQUE: Play note and bend to specified interval. While holding bend, tap onto note indicated.

LEGATO SLIDE: Play note and slide to the following note. (Only first note is attacked).

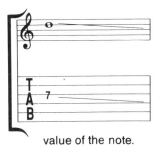

LONG GLISSANDO: Play note and slide in specified direction for the full value of the note.

SHORT GLISSANDO: Play note for its full value and slide in specified direction at the last possible moment.

PICK SLIDE: Slide the edge of the pick in specified direction across the length of the string(s).

MUTED STRINGS: A percussive sound is made by laying the fret hand across all six strings while pick hand strikes specified area (low, mid, high strings).

PALM MUTE: The note or notes are muted by the palm of the pick hand by lightly touching the string(s) near the bridge.

TREMOLO PICKING: The note or notes are picked as fast as possible.

TRILL: Hammer on and pull off consecutively and as fast as possible between the original note and the grace note.

ACCENT: Notes or chords are to be played with added emphasis.

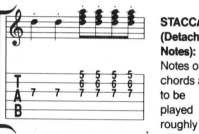

STACCATO (Detached Notes): Notes or chords are to be played roughly half their actual value and with separation.

DOWN STROKES AND UPSTROKES: Notes or chords are to be played with either a downstroke (⊓) or upstroke (∨) of the pick.

VIBRATO: The pitch of a note is varied by a rapid shaking of the fret hand finger, wrist, and forearm.

HARMONICS

NATURAL HARMONIC: A finger of the fret hand lightly touches the note or notes indicated in the tab and is played by the pick hand.

ARTIFICIAL HARMONIC: The first tab number is fretted, then the pick hand produces the harmonic by using a finger to lightly touch the same string at the second tab number (in parenthesis) and is then picked by another finger.

ARTIFICIAL "PINCH" HAR-MONIC: A note is fretted as indicated by the tab, then the pick hand produces the harmonic by squeezing the pick firmly while using the tip of the index finger in the pick attack. If parenthesis are found around the fretted note, it does not sound. No parenthesis means both the fretted note and A.H. are heard simultaneously.

TREMOLO BAR

SPECIFIED INTERVAL: The pitch of a note or chord is lowered to a specified interval and then may or may not return to the original pitch. The activity of the tremolo bar is graphically represented by peaks and valleys.

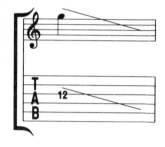

UN-SPECIFIED INTERVAL: The pitch of a note or a chord is lowered to an unspecified interval.